BOSTON HARBOR

Eric Wiberg

by the same author:

U-Boats in New England
U-Boats off Bermuda
U-Boats in the Bahamas
Mailboats of the Bahamas
Bahamas in World War II
Drifting to the Duchess (book)
Drifting (script, with Paolo Pilladi)
Round the World in the Wrong Season
Tanker Disasters
Published Writing
Juvenilia
Swan Sinks
Tankers East of Suez
Napoleon's Battles (with Felix Wiberg)
Åke Wiberg (with Mats Larsson)

Published by Island Books, Boston, MA, USA

© Eric Troels Wiberg, 2020

ISBN: 978-0-9994378-6-5

Library of Congress Control Number: 2020900404

All rights reserved. No part of this publication may be reproduced in any manner without the prior written permission of the publisher, except in the case of brief quotations embodied in articles or reviews. All photographs and text are the exclusive creation of the author, who asserts his rights to them under both national and international copyright and intellectual property laws.

For information, or to contact the author please email eric@ericwiberg.com.

Design and layout by Abdul Rehman Qureshi writingpanacea@gmail.com

Printed in the United States of America

for Caitlin D. Fitzgerald

TABLE OF CONTENTS

ACKNOWLEDGEMENTS VII

FOREWORD IX

INTRODUCTION 1

MAPS OF BOSTON HARBOR 7

VIEWS OF BOSTON'S HARBOR 9

BIG BOATS ON BOSTON HARBOR 30

WATER TAXIS OF BOSTON HARBOR 66

SUNRISE & SUNSET ON BOSTON HARBOR 96

BIRDS, DUCKS & DUCKLINGS 105

LIFE ON THE HARBOR 108

RANDOM SCENES ON BOSTON HARBOR 118

WINTER ON BOSTON HARBOR 138

EAST BOSTON 152

BOSTON HARBOR ON THE EVE OF THE CORONAVIRUS LOCKDOWN 165

ABOUT THE AUTHOR 167

ACKNOWLEDGEMENTS

I thank the many persons who have provided me the training and support and comradery to enjoy the job on the water as much as I do and make it safer to boot. I thank Caitlin, Kent and Petra and family. As well as my employers, without whom most of these photographs could not have been taken. I specifically wish to thank all of my fellow captains; the women and men, who have taught me the ropes, borne my conversation, and often picked up the VHF to agree to let our little vessels pass. I also thank Ryan, Bill, Chris, Miss Ellie, Anita, Tim, Joyce, Two Brothers, Angela's and Canton Eatery. Be well, Alex, and Felix, I hope that you are proud of Daddy. Finally, I thank every passenger I had the privilege to transport safely and I hope merrily, whether they were locals, commuters, colleagues, or visitors from faraway lands with harbors of their own.

FOREWORD

Boston Harbor has an extraordinary story to tell. Its very size brought the colonists to its shores. Its location inspired the building of a city. Its limitations resulted in a 75% expansion of the city claiming some of that harbor. A lack of care and attention to its water quality dramatically affected the city; however subsequent care and attention brought a modern renaissance to its waterfront. Today Boston's harbor front is barely recognizable from even 20 years ago.

In the mid 20th century Boston Harbor was one of the dirtiest harbors in the country. You needed a tetanus shot just to work there. 50 years of trash dumped on Spectacle Island burned for ten years. Floating sewage washed ashore on the harbor beaches. No one wanted anything to do with the harbor. An elevated highway was built through downtown effectively cutting off the harbor from the city. When citizens sued the city for the cleanup of their harbor a federal judge decreed that a sewage treatment plant be built whereupon Boston's Harbor transformation was underway. The elevated highway became a tunnel beneath the city, effectively reuniting the citizenry with their harbor. The islands are being cleaned up and are now the Boston Harbor Islands National Park. The old homes with tiny waterfront windows stand next to the new condos with floor to ceiling windows that proclaim the harbor is now something to seek out and celebrate.

Many historical events and transformations are still evident from the harbor perspective if you hop on a little boat and travel around the many serendipitous nooks and crannies, the wharves and piers, the completely transformed waterfront of South Boston, the 43 mile Boston Harborwalk, all demonstrating the impact on a city and its people a harbor can have over time, and vice versa. Or you could just thumb through this book from the comfort of your couch. These are working photos telling the story of industry, production, and real life, not beautiful photographs telling of beauty. The author doesn't claim to be a professional photographer. He's a boat captain using photography to show his story rather than tell it through the inadequacy of words. And yet that is the beauty of these photographs; the working stories they tell and the way they ignite the viewer's imagination. Have you spent countless weeks on an oil tanker? Have you spent a cold February day in the snow and sleet on a water taxi driving business people from one shoreline dock to another? How about on a car carrier ship with 8,000 cars coming into port for delivery? Ever been a tug or a pilot boat captain? A drawbridge operator? Spent time on a stern dragger fishing now for underutilized species as the historic cod stock dwindles?

Spending time on a boat on Boston Harbor is a virtual trip through time. The USS Constitution, the oldest commissioned warship afloat in the world, is docked here just down the hill from the Bunker Hill Monument and across the way from historic Old North Church. In between church and ship stands the iconic cable-stayed "Zakim" bridge, designed as a motif for both the monument and the rigging of the ship, as it spans the mouth of the Charles River from Charlestown to Boston. Currently docked in Boston are two historic Nantucket Lightships, one a floating museum, the other a refurbished floating condo (for sale). From the wharves of the early 1700's standing the test of time to the dilapidated piers giving in to the harshness of that time; from the people, the great ships, the work boats and pleasure craft, to the working waterfront commingling with historic landmarks, the condominiums, the public open spaces, 8 beaches, 34 islands, the businesses and international airport, the aforementioned fortuitous treatment facility, and on through the neighborhoods, cheek by jowl the history is rich and plentiful. As Captain Eric takes his passengers from dock to dock on his floating "office", we, from the comfort of our recliner, are invited to sit back and let him serve as our illustrative tour guide of Boston Harbor. Through the eye of a boat captain plying his trade through one of this country's oldest working harbors our captain offers you a photo essay through the layers of time.

Fair Winds and a Following Sea.

David Coffin

INTRODUCTION

No camera tripod was used in the making of this book. Nor was a "camera" in the traditional sense, and nor was a professional photographer utilized. The author is not an expert on Boston history or even its ancient maritime traditions. Rather he's a waterborne working upstart who thought this would be a nice thank-you gift to his employers around Christmastime. What these images and captions lack in studied framing and staging, they make up for immediacy and authenticity. Rarely were there more than 3-5 seconds to capture a vessel in the right light, at the right distance and angle, as often both vessels were moving in opposite directions.

I took thousands of images largely alone on a working passenger boat, and was fortunate to even get the subject boats in frame for long enough for my iPhone7 to capture them. The rustic, varnished appearance may make purists shudder, for many of the rest of us will appreciate that these are "the real thing," and in real time, with a lot of moving parts at play and other more important things to do. I get a chuckle out of the thought that after publishing over 3 million words in many mediums and several languages since 1980, this book, which has almost no words, may actually be the most popular! For the audience's sake, I hope so.

The photos are taken literally from the inside, by a vessel captain who works alone in a little cocoon. While the photographer worked alone, in reality he was well supported, operating in close tandem with a team of other captains, who then interact with dispatchers, supervisors, and the captains of myriad other craft.

Those craft include survey boats to whale watchers, tugs, push-boats, oil-supply boats (called bunker barges), others carrying distillates like ethanol, some anchored, some public safety boats whizzing by well lit, others rowing, or in fast dinghies, paddle boards, electric-powered boards, and little Sunfish. These, meanwhile were all being dodged by ferries to Hingham, Hull, Provincetown, Salem, the casino in Everett, commuter boats to Lovejoy and Constitution Wharf; massive cruise ships, LNG tankers, product tankers and articulated tug and barges; all in a day's work, and more. Every time the boat left the dock the fleet owners, managers, US Coast Guard, and thanks to vessel satellite tracking technology, knew how many were on board, where they were leaving from, and to where bound. That is reassuring.

These photographs were taken in and around Boston Harbor, from the Tobin Bridge eastward to the start of the Boston Harbor Islands National and State Park, to Winthrop, Deer Island, East Boston, Black Falcon Terminal and the Seaport District to the Fort Point area around the Boston Tea Party re-enactment ships, the Financial District, North End, TD Garden, Charlestown, and around to Chelsea and Whidden's Point, to East Boston, where the waterfront is in a high degree of flux.

The idea for this project came on a whim as a way to thank my employers for giving me a chance to get back on the water as the captain of a smallish passenger vessel going to 25 different piers and docks, made of stone, steel, and wood, around Boston Harbor. My fellow captains and I start out solo before dawn and have two shifts going till 10 in the night, in all weather, year-round. I started taking photos of birds, seals, old wharves, new and old buildings and so on. I shied away from photos of people out of professional courtesy, and because this book celebrates a workaday way of life which is new to many readers; and yet which employs thousands of men and women on the water, most of them federally licensed, whether ship's pilots, deckhands, cooks or servers, or captains.

The daily commuters are part of Boston's waterborne fabric. This book is not about a waterfront so much as being on the water itself; seeing the City of Boston and it's people and their myriad activities from the water itself; away from shore, yet part of it, and helping it's people get to and from work, from the airport, hospitals, sports games and concerts, hotels and marinas. For several passengers it is the first time in a boat, and for many it is a very special time of their day, month, or year. We witness marriage proposals, and take people to weddings as well as wakes: I watched as a passenger jumped off the boat onto a dock, hugged his brother and immediately transformed into Best Man as his brother's marriage, initiated in Belize, was promptly solemnized there on the jetty!

By way of background, I began a 30-year maritime career with racing sailboats for Boston College on the Charles River and around Logan Airport, then racing in Annapolis and later, to Bermuda. Over the years I raced and delivered some 130 vessels, mostly sailboats, as well as power, to many countries, from New Zealand to Sweden. Then I became a fleet operator of tanker ships from Singapore, with a dabble in dry-bulks ships. Study of maritime law and ocean policy ensured, then a varied career mostly sales roles representing salvage tugs and barges and workboats, and tractor tugs.

Working for a leading bulk shipping newspaper covering every kind of commercial watercraft enabled me to travel widely, mostly between Athens and Vancouver. Seven years as a part-time launch driver taking folks between their boats and shore in Newport for Oldport Marine during graduate school sparked an idea when I returned to Boston unexpectedly to be near my son in mid-2019. As I explored Boston Harbor from a base on Eagle Hill in East Boston, I was drawn to the types of equipment which people operate around the clock in Boston Harbor, including bridges, dredges, fire boats and police boats.

There are whole teams working as engineers on the vessels and buildings, as bridge operators and dispatchers, on payroll and balancing the day's revenues, calling from hotels to send passengers aboard, and graciously providing places of shelter and relief to mariners around the harbor. Without them, the boats and their captains could not operate, providing a region without pipelines with its fuel and gas for all rolling stock, cars, trucks, planes, and gas for building and oil for power generation. I was flummoxed to learn that a single – one of many – marine fuel dock requires 10 trucks of diesel a day in the busy summer!

This book aims to be unusual; there is very little text, as the images are meant to be self-explanatory. Themes such as weather, geography, wind, snow, rain, fog and dark all become characters of sorts, as do the vessels themselves. Often the vessels being photographed are difficult to distinguish against the buildings and maritime clutter. That is intentional; these different industrial craft are part of the fabric, yet also to many are invisible. Though the reader cannot hear the VHF radios cackle, and the slap of a ship's wake hitting one's boat, or the wind lifting and dropping awnings like the sigh of bellows, and the churn of a faithful propeller around the debris which is a constant threat to all except the biggest ships, the hope is that the images will provide some kind of tactile experience and exposure.

There is a bit of the wide-eyed-wonder of *Katie and Big Snow* or *Mike Mulligan and His Steam Shovel* by Virginia Lee Burton, in this narrative. In April I moved to East Boston from the West Village in Manhattan where I'd been writing about German submarines besieging New England and leaving five never-found TMC-type mines between Graves Island and Nahant. I left Boston before the Big Dig was completed and was astounded at the difference between seeing the water taxi 'wars' off Logan Airport (which MassPort ably suppressed), in the early 2000's and the fall months between August and mid-December in 2019. It is like a city revitalized, and utilizing the water to connect rather than separate its populace and many visitors.

Boston Harbor is an extraordinary and busy and lively and commercial place. It is also a danger-fraught region of the nations' waterways where global mega-ships carrying cargoes that range from cars to Egyptian salt to gypsum intermingle with cross-harbor water-taxis and water workers of all stripes and dialects in all conditions, dark, foggy, and bright. The several radio frequencies convey a myriad of accents from far eastern to colloquial Boston and Charlestown; Braintree and the Bayou and maritime academies all mixed, whether raising a bridge or requesting permission to pass, or inquiring whether a certain boat may have cables out, that might trip up your boat.

The central characters of this book are not buildings, but boats; not people so much as the weather they are constantly adjusting to. There is a cycle at play; on a summer afternoon it seems like a delicate ballet as unspoken rules allow a dozen boats to untangle from a wharf without hitting each other. That cycle can turn brutal as smaller vessels struggle against three-or-four-foot waves, four runs of powerful current daily, each at least nine feet high, debris, radio messages not received, very cold conditions, challenging lack of visibility, and pure tedium.

But please remember that no one in Boston Harbor knows everything, and if they claim to, they probably shouldn't be out there, operating equipment. And boats need to refuel just as those who operate them, so surprising acquaintances can be made at one of the few fuel docks, between enforcers and those being monitored, and vessel operators and the birds and seals they strive to protect from pollution. Odds and ends are found floating in the harbor and taken to a place they are less like to harm other boats, or are taken home as nautical decorations for the mantle, or toys as playthings for children, as you will see.

Boston Harbor is a fascinating place to live and work, as I hope this short slice of images convey.

Note for first edition: No photos were taken before May 2019. Most were taken from August 28 and December 18, 2019. As the book was being prepared by a wonderful team, I kept sending new images of "the one that had gotten away," and of snow and storms and different creatures, like a minke whale, harbor seals, gray seals, bufflehead ducks, eider ducks, and even harbor dolphins that have been sighted. Then in March, as the company and so many others like it was forced to shut down for furlough, as Logan Airport, that pulmonary artery to the seven-state-region's economy, then hotels and wharves started to wind up, and as the shock, fear, and dismay rolled over all of us at the spread of a global pandemic, the outcome of which is still uncertain, this book is published. The last photos were taken on 18 March, since I suddenly had time to walk the waterfront for hours.

Though my team and I (primarily the redoubtable Abdul who has helped bring dozens of books and thousands of pages to light for me) have not produced a color book for wide audiences, we are trying to keep the cost manageable and the book accessible, including releasing it via e-book, Kindle and other means which don't require home delivery in these uncertain, home-bound times. As strange as it may seem in the face of such horror, our genuine intent is to *cheer Boston up!*

So, we are fast-tracking the release on the day the governor called up the National Guard; readers will find many small errors, therefore, and photographers will find so many technical errors their heads will spin. But we want everyone to enjoy this book above all else, and then let's get back on Boston Harbor, and let's get back to work. The harbors and airports brought people and prosperity to Boston, and they will do so again.

Capt. E. T. W., Esq.
Eagle Hill, East Boston
March 20, 2020

MAPS OF BOSTON HARBOR

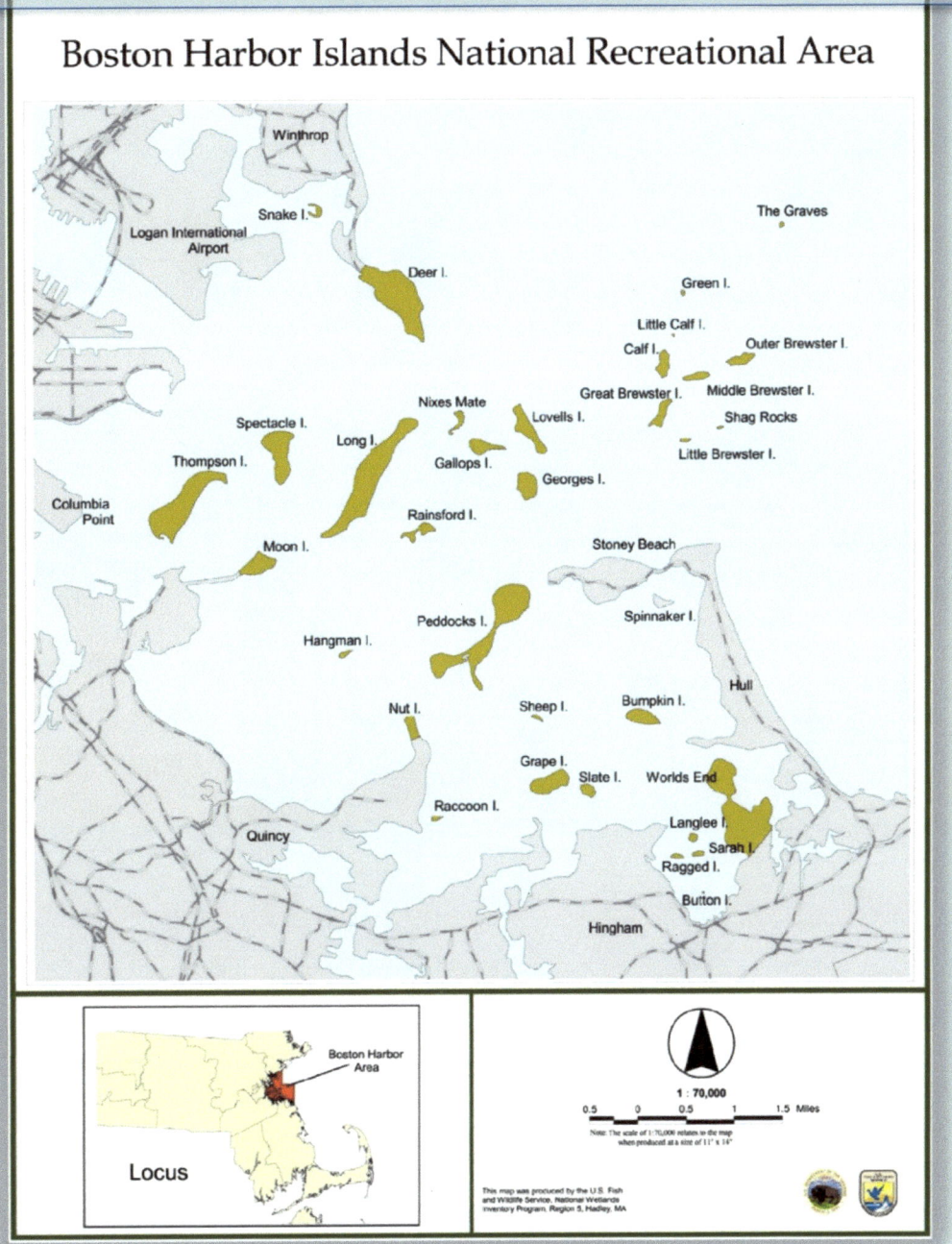

Source: Public Domain; en.wikipedia.org/wiki/Boston_Harbor_Islands_National_Recreation_Area#/media/File:Boston_Harbor_Islands_National_Recreation_Area.png

Locations of the port

Functions of the port

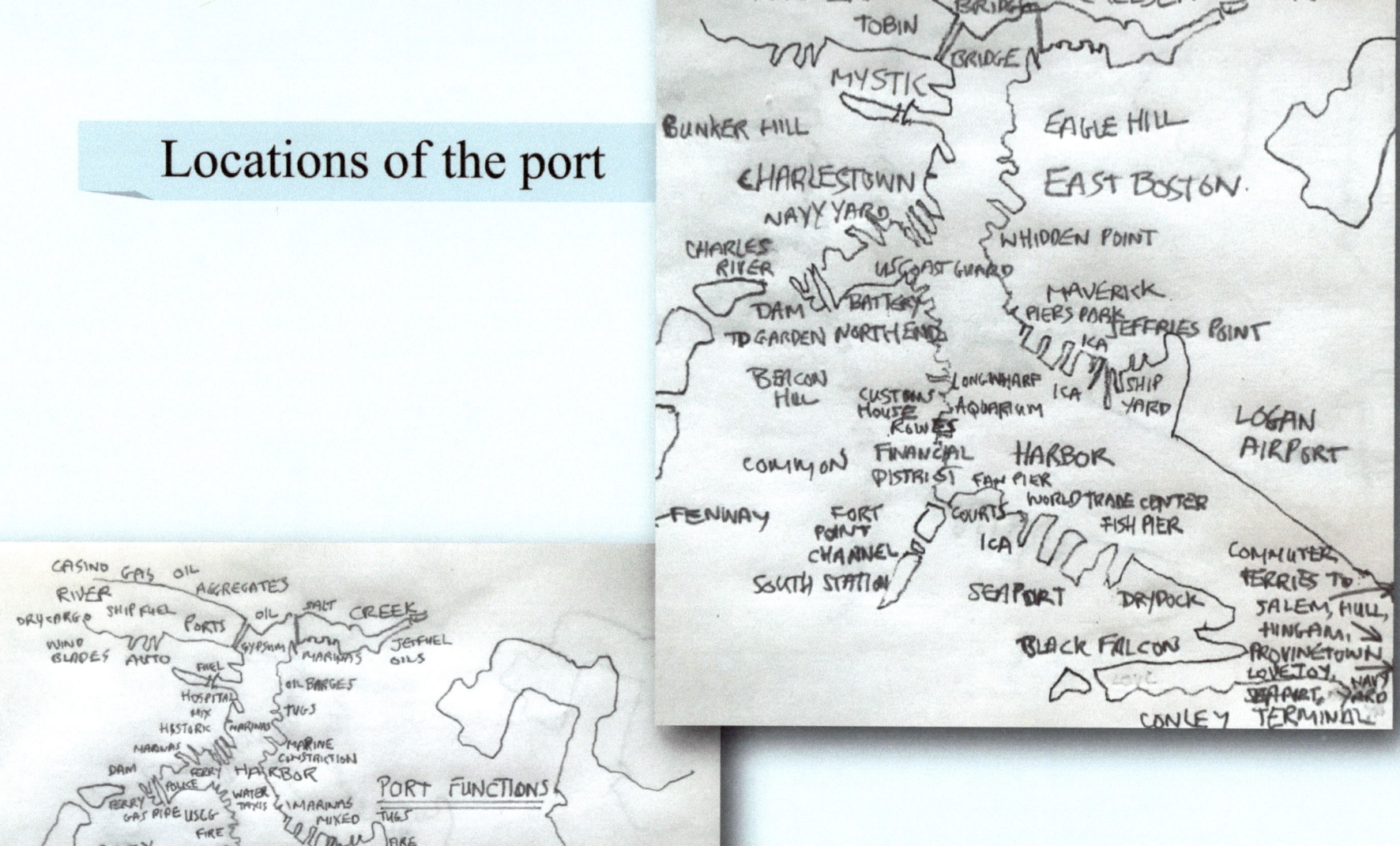

VIEWS OF BOSTON HARBOR

Boston from Piers Park, East Boston, from the East Boston Harborside Community Center, from the Hyatt Regency Boston Harbor.

East Boston from the Battery Wharf, near the US Coast Guard, from Long Wharf to Columbus Park, Commercial Wharf, and from Massport's Headquarters.

Boston and Charlestown from East Boston's Eagle Hill

From Hyatt Boston Harbor and of Long Wharf, downtown, of the Customs House overlooking Aquarium.

A lobster boat fishing the clean harbor passing an ethanol barge pushed by the Kirby Corporation tug Denali

John Joseph Moakley US Courthouse, with Vertex Pharmaceuticals' office tower.

City skyline, with a bird in flight from Spectacle Island, one of over 30 in Boston Harbor Islands State Park

Pollution boom around new construction; Maverick, East Boston, looking at North End, Battery, USCG base, Leonard P. Zakim Bunker Hill Memorial Bridge

Boston from the Customs House tower, now Marriott, and view of Winthrop westwards towards Chelsea Creek Bridge in background.

Intercontinental Boston, Fort Point between Congress Street and Seaport Boulevard bridges and opposite the Boston Children's Museum.

Rowes Wharf

From Eagle Hill East Boston, with brightest lights at USCG base in the North End

Charles River, dammed off from Boston Harbor, offers many recreational small boat experiences

Here a DUCK Boat heads towards the Museum of Science. One of the Boston Tea Party re-enactment boats, the *Beaver*

Many jurisdictions offer first responder and other public services: above is a Massport fire boat serving primarily Logan Airport, and below a buoy tender by the USCG. The boat at right is a crew boat bringing crew ashore and to and from industrial dredging and other operations nearshore and offshore.

The Institute of Contemporary Art and Pier Four Boulevard residences near the Fan Piers, with Goodwin law firm offices above.

From Charlestown's former navy yard.

A Reinauer Transportation Co. tug and barge, light or in ballast, outbound in winter.

Old rail terminal between the Institute of Contemporary Art and Piers Park Sailing Center, and the Boston Harbor Shipyard & Marina.

Soccer ball, probably from LoPresti Park, where it is played almost continuously, and Pier Four Boulevard residences overlooking the ICA near Fan Pier and the World Trade Center at the Seaport.

From Fort Warren, George's Island

BIG BOATS ON BOSTON HARBOR

Irving Oil of Saint John, New Brunswick, Canada, imports much of the petroleum products which Bostonians consume. The tankers are virtually custom built to squeeze through the McArdle Bridge from the harbor to Chelsea Creek, making them long and narrow. Their names: *Nor'easter* and *New England* reflect the ship's dedication to the route. Here the gangway is down ready to release a pilot, the boilers are adding pressure as seen by the steam emitting above the funnel, the letter "V" on the bow indicates the ship and crew are managed by the V-Ships firm of Aberdeen, Scotland and Monaco. Tankers are flush-decked with just derrick for lifting and lowering the cargo hoses, usually 10-ton safe-working load. The numbers and size and purpose of each manifold is painted on the side below the derrick; it looks as though this ship can carry over 8 separate products and the smaller circles indicate gasoil and other fuels required by the ship for the engines; with new regulations against Sulphur emissions meaning the thick marine fuel oil is rarely used close to populations.

This is *Nantucket* Lightship MLV612, operational from when built in 1950 to 1983. She was purchased in 2000 by Bill and Kristen Golden, who contributed his legal skill and persistence to the cleanup of Boston Harbor. The couple have extensively refurbished her interior to top-notch condition, and it is for sale.

Irving Oil's tankers *New England* and *Nor'Easter*, registered to the Marshall Islands and escorted by Reinauer tugs. Note the modern lifeboats ready to deploy with the help of gravity, unlike the antiquated models aboard the US-flagged El Faro, sunk in Hurricane Joaquin in 2015 with the loss of all mariners.

Encore casino in Everett custom-built lovely power yachts to shuttle guests from Seaport, Long Wharf and East Boston's Whidden Point. The wall of a ship on lower right is a car carrier, sister to the *Cougar Ace*, owned by Mitsui OSK which lost stability off the Aleutian Islands, Alaska with the loss of one surveyor in 2006.

The tug *Ocean King* was built in 1950 and was *Resolute* and *David McAllister* before Patriot Marine of Winthrop renamed her. Her predecessor, also *Ocean King*, was witness to the last German U-boat attack ever, by U-853 off Point Judith, Rhode Island, against the *Black Point*. I interviewed one of her young crew, who fled the scene, in 2018, 3 days before he passed. That tug, also named *Chaplain*, *Margaret Sheridan*, and *Carina*, is believed searching for oil and gas in the Bahamas for a Las Vegas entity.

The *J. W. Powell* lower right may (or may not) have also been the former Ivy Trawler named *Harvard*, built as a steam trawler in 1926 at 179 feet long. She patrolled the North Atlantic fishery until 1941 when she became the US Navy *Bellefonte*, and in 1944 became *Albatross* for the Woods Hole Oceanographic Institute. Last dusted off in around 2005 for a hunt for non-existent treasure on the British U-boat victim *Port Nicholson* off Cape Cod, she has been languishing since.

Passenger pleasure cruise vessel

Commuter Boat

To the Boston Harbor Islands,
    all ages aboard!

To and from Long Wharf, Logan Aiport, Hingham, Hull or Salem.
To the lower right, those are water taxi captains in the midst of a crew shift change.

37

Here come the new crop of captains above, and below the commuters arrive beneath the Customs House; built tall so revenue scouts could observe all activities, built of stone so the taxed didn't torch it. Now a Marriott resort, cameras allow the public to observe a family of nesting peregrine falcons.

Two product tankers provide the lifeline of petroleum to regional airports, gas stations and beyond. Both have discharged their cargo and are high out of the water and in ballast as they head outbound with pilots on board (red and white flags behind mast). Above *Great Eastern* is owned by Irving and named for the largest ship afloat in 1858, built in London by Isambard Kingdom Brunel. *High Explorer* by D'Amico International Shipping of Italy.

Great Eastern and two Reinauer (Boston Towing and Transportation) tugs creeping through a foggy dawn towards Chelsea Creek.

The large red bulk ship (no gears or derrick, flush deck, 7 cargo holds for dry cargo) exits Boston past Fan Pier Park and Rowe's Wharf in light, or ballast condition. Navios is a successful publicly traded company formed from US Steel which is now run by Ms. Angeliki Frangou in Athens Greece.

You know its blowing a bad gale when the Cashman Dredging barges and dredges return to port and anchor off Jeffries Point to ride it out. Here they are; big contributors to the Big Dig and home grown.

Caledonia is a hermaphrodite brigantine brought in as an entertainment venue for local restaurateurs. By 2020 it hopes to be open for business on the East Pier, Maverick, East Boston, near Portside East Pier.

An Irving tanker is two thirds through the narrow McArdle Bridge into Chelsea Creek, with a tug at either end tethered and assisting.

A dry bulk ship owned by the largest ship owner in the world, COSCO, for China Ocean Shipping Company, passes The Eddy at Whidden Point, with Flagship Wharf and Parris Landing residential complexes at the Charlestown Navy Yard in the background.

Tankers being wedged into and out of Chelsea Creek via McArdle Bridge, before and to the north of the Maurice J. Tobin Memorial Bridge.

Below is one of the larger catamarans, *Salacia*, usually on the Provincetown ferry run but in the winter filling in between Hull and Hingham and Boston.

Large product, or chemical tanker passing North End inbound, the Norwegian car carrier owned by Wallenius Wilhelmsen having discharged European or Japanese automobiles at the autopier in Mystic River, passing the Rockland Trust Bank Pavilion and former Army building, now Reebok, and a gas carrier from the venerated old shipping firm Knutsen O. A. S. of Haugesund, Norway, *Iberica Knutsen* arrives under close escort past Logan to discharge at the Mystic Generating Station between Admirals Hill and Malden Bridge in Everett.

New England arriving in a January dawn

Glory shuttling into the Massport passenger terminal which connects air travellers heading into the city with others being dropped off at Logan or the Hyatt Regency Boston Harbor by water taxi, private launch, crew boat, tugboat tender, or commuter ferries like the *Glory*.

Some examples of movements which often go undetected: a crane being shifted by the Patriot Marine tug *Ocean King* from the Seaport back to East Boston. The USCG Cutter *Seneca* returning to base in North End with a standby tug from Boston Towing & Transportation, which though owned by a Staten Island New York parent company, boasts 155 years of service in Boston and has eight tugboats, many of them ultra-modern tractor tugs designed to spin on a dime and "transverse arrest" to stop ships by being dragged sideways. Below is one of two Canadian warships visiting the city, with the Washington Street Bridge behind and Zakim Bridge framing. The Washington Street Bridge connects the North End with Charlestown and its replacement is made more challenging by the fact it carries the main gas line from Everett into Boston.

The fishing dragger *Flight I* at the Fish Piers, the elegant *Provincetown II* tied up at the World Trade Center in the Seaport across the narrow channel, and tugs tied up at the Boston Harbor Shipyard and Marina at Jeffries Point, which shares space with marinas, a marine fuel facility and the Institute of Contemporary Art.

The Liberian-flagged oil products tanker *SCF Ussuri* was built in 2009 and is here leaving Boston past the Tobin Bridge, the Customs House, and the Autoport in Charlestown (the grey and red-striped building at bottom left, with gypsum silos looming over).

USCGC *Spencer* (WMEC 905) is 270 feet and was built in Middletown, RI in 1982. Since then she was in the Perfect Storm rescue, commanded the EgyptAir 1990 search and recovery effort off Nantucket, towed a large disabled US Navy frigate to shore, and rescued many from a ferry sinking in Haiti in 1993. On top of WWII-related Fleet Week activities, her 100 personnel have performed numerous rescues of thousands of floating immigrants, many of them Haitian or Cuban, made 23 high-seas arrests, and countless cocaine and marijuana interdictions off Venezuela, Honduras, Panama, and beyond; those symbols painted on the bridge wing above the letter "E" are of marijuana leaves and bales of cocaine intercepted. Armed with 76 mm and .50 caliber machine and naval guns as well as Dolphin, Jayhawk and Stingray helicopters housed in a hangar aft, she is based on Hanover and Commercial Streets (where most captains on Boston Harbor obtain and maintain their US Merchant Mariner licenses), the *Spencer* has been affectionately nicknamed Cellblock 905 by her crew.

Below is *Hellas Aphrodite,* a Maltese-flagged, Greek-owned double-hull oil and chemical tanker built in 2016 of 50,000 cargo-carrying tons, inbound with the Hilton at Logan Airport in background.

An ATB, or Articulated Tug and Barge unit (oil barge with a U-shaped notch at the back for a tug to insert into), approaching Chelsea Creek past Charlestown, from East Boston. It is cheaper to man a tug boat than a ship, so the tug temporarily takes over several barges.

Another product tanker outbound in ballast, two tugs passing their base in East Boston, to lower right.

The large Norwegian gas carrier being backed under the Tobin Bridge (barely) with heavy military and police escort, Whidden Point East Boston in foreground: all other marine traffic halts during these movements to Everett.

Tug *Baltic Dawn* with its bridge in a tower for higher height-of-eye is refueling in winter, with an abandoned kid's inflatable raft all that remains of a recreational dock till summer.

Looking up White Street at Boston Towing & Transportation (Reinauer)'s base on Border Street, East Boston. On that site renowned shipwright Donald McKay and his team built the fastest ships afloat, including *Flying Cloud*, *Sovereign of the Seas*, and *Lightning* between 1845 and 1869. Designs included extreme clippers, packet ships, and what are known as famine ships.

The Patriot Marine tug fleet in the Boston Harbor Shipyard and Marina, Jeffries Point, also in East Boston. USCG patrol and enforcement craft with an ATB in background, looking at Logan from the Fish Piers.

51

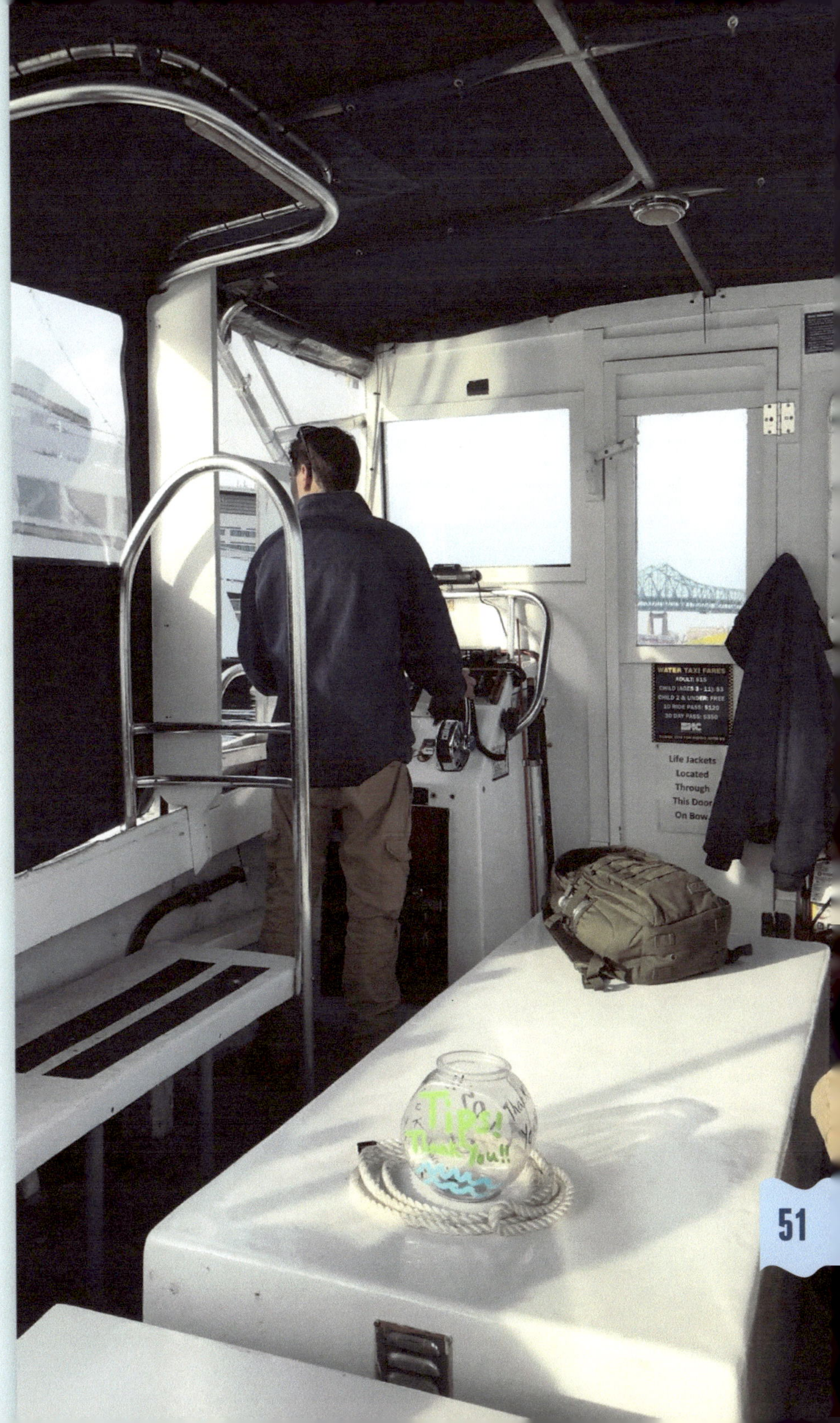

The USS *Constitution*, *Old Ironsides*, was built in 1797 and is the planet's oldest commissioned naval vessel afloat. Battle tested many times over, she is a national and world treasure and sails from a protected pen in Charlestown, beneath the Bunker Hill Monument, very rarely. Here a late-summer voyage has been put on for a special group of history teachers on a sunny day. *Moira Smith* and her sister ships carry commuters from between the Zakim and Washington Street bridges at Lovejoy to the ICA at the Seaport. The currents from Charles River water released by the dam around the clock, plus construction to replace the Washington Street Bridge make this a very trick place to dock, so the crew have placed their own flags on the pilings so they can see them and the wind speed and direction. Note the white water emitted under the vessel bow near the State Police marine base: that's flowing out of the dam into a very confined construction site with barges and cranes always shifting.

Tug *Justice* returning from escorting a ship outbound

Laid up near the World Trade Center in the Seaport

Passenger ferry *Salacia* refueling of the ICA in Eastie, with the push boat *Bumper* from Harbor Fuels in foreground and the other *Nantucket Lightship*, LV-112, which served from 1936 to 1983 and is now a museum open to visitors.

A tanker at anchor off Deer Island Wastewater Treatment Plant, with Long Island in the background. Note the stumps to the right of and behind the tanker: those are the remains of a bridge which connected Moon Island to Long Island from Quincy and Dorchester. The island's history since 1634 is too long for this caption; most recently it housed persons without homes and in recovery, but in 2015 the bridge had to be destroyed as unsafe. Still in use for farming, access is now by boat.

The lean, rugged and fast Pilot boat must make it to the bottom of a gangway in the high seas outside the harbor and stay alongside long enough for a ship's pilot with a satchel to safely jump onto the gangway or ladder and begin - or end - a precipitous climb.

Tug under way and the unusual tug's wheelhouse used as a landmark at the mixed-use ICA and Boston Harbor Shipyard facility.

Painted from navy blue to white, the brig *Caledonia*, a 203-foot, three-masted brigantine moved from Toronto to Boston for the Navy Yard Hospitality group in May of 2019. The new owners, who have Pier 6 in Charlestown, and the Reel House in East Boston and South Boston, are hoping to open its gangway to diners and events in East Boston.

Tug *Linda Moran* of Moran Towing Corporation, New Canaan, Connecticut, with its barge at anchor awaiting its turn off Jeffries Point to enter Chelsea Creek.

Five dragger-type fishing boats, the 2nd and 3rd in the same fleet, at the Boston Fish Pier, with the Renaissance Boston Waterfront Hotel in background. Though No Name Seafood, run by a kindly gentleman of Greek descent, recently closed, Legal Seafoods and other establishments thrive.

Tug *Baltic Dawn* has come into port from engineering support work outside the harbor, and has a crew boat in green behind it at the Harbor Fuels floating depot. The white, yellow and blue vessel is a bunker barges which is pushed by the pushboat named *Bumper* in the background over to mid-size vessels which then take on fuel, or bunkers, for their engines from it.

Bottom to the left the motor vessel *Fintry*, to the right the *Nantucket Lightship LV-112* which replaced the lightship which was run over and sunk by the *SS Olympic* (Titanic's sister ship) with the loss of 7 lives. In the left background are vents for the tunnels under the harbor and the far right are the ship container cranes at Conley Terminal in southie.

Clockwise from left: the pushboat *Edward X. McDevitt* brings in the barges and equipment needed to renew and expand the World Trade Center.

A dragger shows where the spools of needs are passed through the middle of the stern, with the large stabilizers standing upright amishups.

A Reinauer ATB on a calm dawn waits and anchor to discharge product; possibly ethanol, jetfuel, or petroleum additives from as far away as Houston, Port Arthur, or the Port of New York and New Jersey, which offer the nearest US refinery capacity to Boston.

USCG base and the Old North Church

There are many vessels in this image, the one with ET on the stack is thought to be the former *Eric R. Thornton*, which had been the 1960-built Rhode Island tug *Roger Williams*, for a time owned by the author's former employers the McAllister family. Presently believed to be the *Preston James* and owned by Legacy Marine Incorporated, getting access to two fleets of tugs from shore can be complicated, as it is mixed-use arts and industrial and one has to prove a reason to gain access to the shipyard.

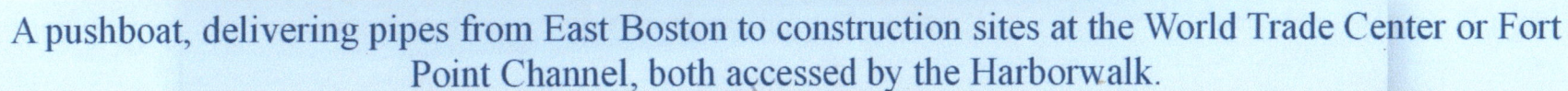

A pushboat, delivering pipes from East Boston to construction sites at the World Trade Center or Fort Point Channel, both accessed by the Harborwalk.

A geared bulk carrier (note the grab buckets between the cranes), owned by the China Ocean Shipping Corporation (COSCO: with over 1,000 ships the largest fleet in the world), rounds Whidden Point laden with road salt either from Bahamas, Egypt or Chile.

A large black dock float drifting around off Charlestown Marina in front of the passenger vessel *Majestic*

Tanker *High Explorer* heads back to sea.

Offshore wind support vessel Scarlett Isabella, from the US Gulf but now Boston-owned, heads to sea. During migrations of the Right Whale and others at Stellwagen Bank, Nantucket, and Rhode Island Sound, speeds are carefully monitored and restricted with strict penalties. When I was in grad school students were paid to monitor, document, enforce whale watch boats while posing as tourists.

The 1985-built *Gateway Endeavor* is an offshore supply vessel (OSV) utilized in supporting the nascent offshore wind energy sector largely being led by northern European firms. On the first day of each month all USCG-inspected vessels are required to test their fire-fighting and other rescue capabilities, and here is the *Gateway Endeavor* testing her fire hoses.

Tugboat with a rather Mediterranean name: *Aegean Sea*, at Mystic in Charlestown; part of the fleet of one of several small marine engineering firms in the area.

Bulk ship discharging salt in Chelsea Creek across the Andrew McArdle Bridge connecting Chelsea and East Boston.

The USS *Constitution*, veteran of the Barbary Pirate wars, and the USS *Cassin Young*, a US Navy destroyer from 1943 to 1974 and World War II veteran, in Charlestown.

The newer *Nantucket Lightship* at Charlestown Marina looking towards Constellation Wharf and North End.

Here one sees the ability of vessels like the *Frederick L. Nolan, Jr.,* to "blend in" to the surrounding, as seen down an alley from Long Wharf North to Long Wharf South, with the iconic New England Aquarium in the background, where legendary *Myrtle the Turtle* and so many other aquatic critters reside.

WATER TAXIS OF BOSTON HARBOR

Three water taxis heading out to either set up VHF radios or shovel snow off docks before dawn.

Abandoned private power boat slowly sinking.

Various craft rafted to each other under the McArdle Bridge.

Strong winds may require many lines to hold the boat to the dock, and maybe engine thrust as well.

Massport fire boats preparing to get under way from Jeffries Point.

A bit of humor in Chelsea Creek.

Houseboats in Chelsea Creek on the East Boston side as seen from McArdle Bridge looking to the Chelsea Creek Bridge.

Product tanker anchored off Long Island, with government buildings in background, from Deer Island.

Miss McDevitt is one of many passenger and other vessels which migrate to Boston and surrounding ports - Marblehead, Salem, the Cape - in the summer to carry folks. They range from tall to small sailing boats, floating bars which are pedaled by the patrons, and they arrive from as near as the Charles River and local shipyards and marinas to New York, Maine, Canada, Key West, Bahamas and beyond. Visiting naval and tall ships call from all over the world.

Hangars and slips for various craft in the Little Mystic Channel, Charlestown.

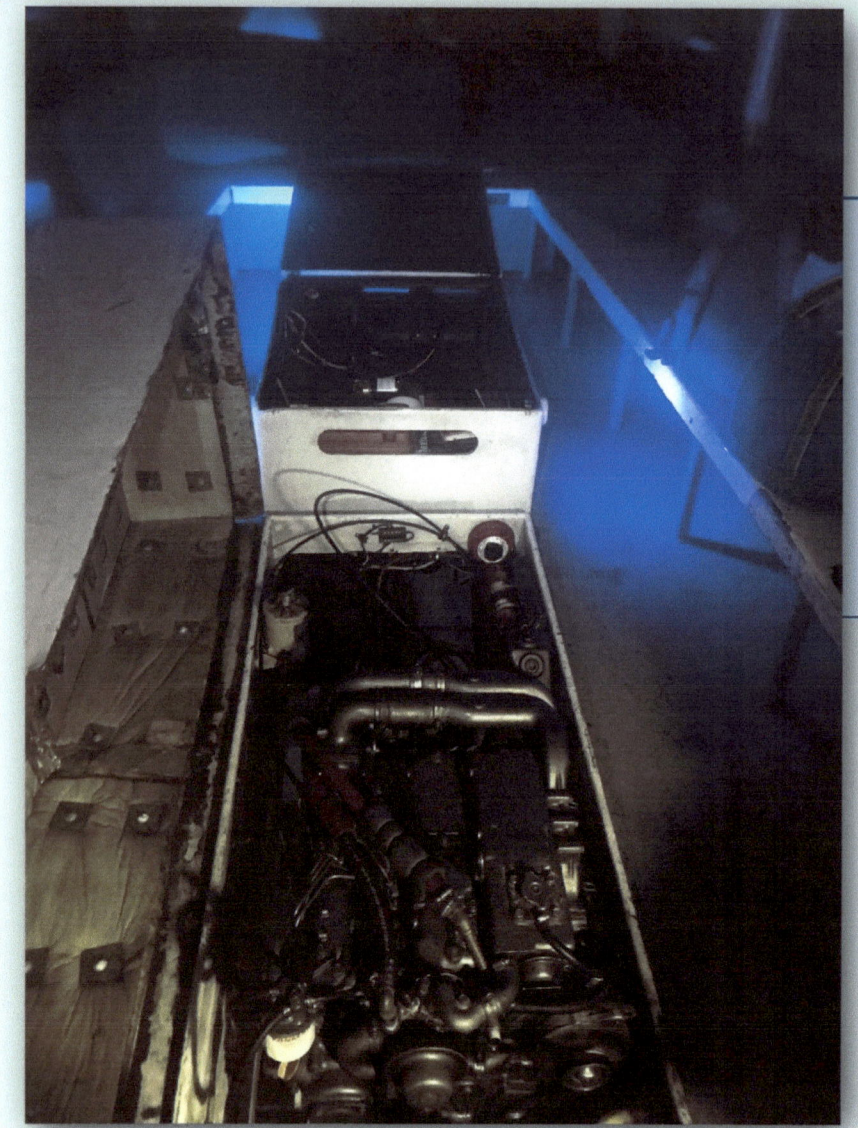

Unless it's an outboard boat, most vessels in Boston Harbor are powered by diesel or marine diesel oil engines. With the hatch open to provide extra warmth to the lone occupant, this shows the "guts" of the boat; a Japanese-made Yanmar marine diesel.

A massive car carrier owned by Glovis heads under the Tobin Bridge towards the Autoport in Charlestown known as the primary Subaru inport facility for the region.

A racing sailing sloop on struts at Boston Shipyard and Marina in Jeffries Point, Eastie.

Boats in repair, on drydock and awaiting deployment or spring at Little Mystic Channel under the Tobin Bridge.

The marina at Harbor Fuels and Boston Harbor Shipyard and Marina; lobster buoys aboard a live-aboard, and the fuel attendant (it happens she is also a US Army veteran) fuels a vessel partly obscured by former USCG patrol craft now servicing the Graves Light Station, owned by David and Lynne Waller, since 2013.

This facility has many uses; seasonal slips, year-round-live-aboards, refueling of tiny gasoline boats to tugs, casino boats and commuter ships. In fact on busy days as many as ten trucks of fuel can make deliveries, and the barge will deliver to ships. Would that New England had a pipeline (the pipeline from Portland to Montreal was built by the Canadians and flows north only).

The USCG stay in the know; they audit and permit or license not only commercial vessels in Boston, but their operators as well. When the author surprised a patrol boat by pouncing out of a darkened channel, they immediately pounced back.

A jack-up or spud barge, with round legs, one of them being lowered from the barge at left.

A single-handed sailor heading out of the harbor in the winter. Two water taxis, the one on the right built by Oldport Marine in Newport, RI, having a "gam" or floating chat between the crew.

A green gas tanker passing Little Mystic Channel.

Water taxis switching crew on 4 or 5 vessels at Long wharf, with the aquarium in the background.

Pushboat with its faithful red runabout boat tied to its side head off to work.

Bumper and her diminutive barge.

The locally-built fleet of 5 luxury craft bringing passengers to the Encore Boston Harbor casino, with stops at Long Wharf and Whidden's Point, Eastie. After passing the Tobin Bridge, if it is high tide, the vessels sometimes have to have the Malden Bridge opened for them.

This is a box to hold VHF radios, backup batteries and other miscellany. They allow customers at a station to simply call for a ride if there is not a boat there already. Given the service lasts till nearly midnight and anyone can call, this has led to some interesting conversations, not all of them about procuring waterborne transportation!

Every weekend at least all winter sailboats set up courses across the harbor and race. Here a boat heading downwind on port tack and wing-and-wing, prepares to round the floating red buoy known as the leeward mark, harden up and head for the windward mark or finish line.

The all-woman crew of an *Encore* boat remove large debris from Long Wharf as a service to other mariners. Consequences from hitting the many pilings, lumber and other jetsam and flotsam can range to glancing blows to shuddering halts and even damage to or removal of propeller shafts, opening the stuffing box between engine space and the harbor, and even sinking.

Captains must always be vigilant for this debris, as Massport disavows responsibility for it, there are four tidal moves a day (2 each way), and often usually rigid radio protocols are relaxed in order for one skipper to warn another of particularly menacing debris.

A vessel out of service under repair for debris-caused damage.

Scenes of sunny Charlestown, Pier 6 and the Courageous Sailing Center. Folks race sailboats pretty much every weekend, year round, rain or shine.

An old-school lobster wholesaler in Fort Point Channel opposite the Barking Crab: James Hook Lobster.

The fearsome adrenaline rush known as *Codzilla* Boat Ride.

Layout of Oldport Marine water taxis

Turkey day in the Little Mystic Channel.

Deer Island from Fort Warren on Georges Island. Simplified; Boston Harbor was a dump for sewage and worse into the mid-1980s. Now with Federal and other funding sewage is treated on Deer Island, which doubles as a lovely long walk from Winthrop.

Many of the Boston Harbor Islands which had been literally trash heaps had the worst layers burned off, capped by mud from the Big Dig, and they were turned into lovely recreational venues for camping, hiking, swimming, fishing, kayaking and day-tripping on private boats or ferries. Win-win. At bottom: A tug boat towing a barge with crane passes a lobster-fishing boat to the right.

A small landing craft to right is passed by the Pilot boat tasked with bringing those experts at local navigation on and off large ships in order to have them manage the tugs, get bridges to open, and dock the ships. They are passing the Battery on North End.

A small workboat passing Whidden Point, Eastie, at dawn. The state Police are admonishing two young men in a Boston Whaler off Portside, East Pier, Maverik, Eastie, for speeding.

If you look carefully this floating Nantucket-shingle office is actually a small powerboat. The "mud room" at right covers outboard engines!.

Fort Point the Seaport, Children's Museum and Boston Tea Party on an island halfway across the Congress Street bridge near South Station.

The basin at Christopher Columbus Waterfront Park, looking from Long Wharf to Commercial Wharf.

Time to offer passengers and captain a dry, enclosed boat.

A Swedish sailor, supported by his wife and first mate, repairs damage done when their boom was broken on a voyage from the St. Lawrence River, Canada to the Bahamas and Caribbean, off Massport at Jeffries Point.

Bumper iced up

Dragger at the Fish Piers.

Returning from whale watching of Stellwagen Bank through the Boston Islands.

Traditional wooden rowing boats at rest beneath the new Seaport Boulevard Bridge at Fort Point Channel near Fan Pier Park.

Water taxis return to base at Little Mystic Channel after 10 pm.

Waiting for diners at Legal Harborside next to the Rockland Trust Bank Pavilion.

5 or more fishing boats at the Fish Piers. Several Boston fishing boats in both world wars survived being shot up by German U-boat submarines and limped back to these exact piers.

Busy channel, Long Wharf.

Repair raft with seagull, Zakim Bridge in background.

A water taxi approaches the airport, Hyatt, Massport, commuter ferry dock in winter.

Taxi heading out of Little Mystic Channel with gypsum silo's behind.

Yacht salvage! A fall storm blew a sailboat off it's mooring near the aquarium, and it banged into a stone jetty till it sank. The next day salvors raised it to prevent obstructing other boats, and the yellow air bags on the right indicate where the dismasted tangle was raised and pumped and towed away.

SUNRISE & SUNSET ON BOSTON HARBOR

Engineering base and layup in Charlestown, with the old Chapman House school on Eagle Hill, Eastie, in background with chimneys.

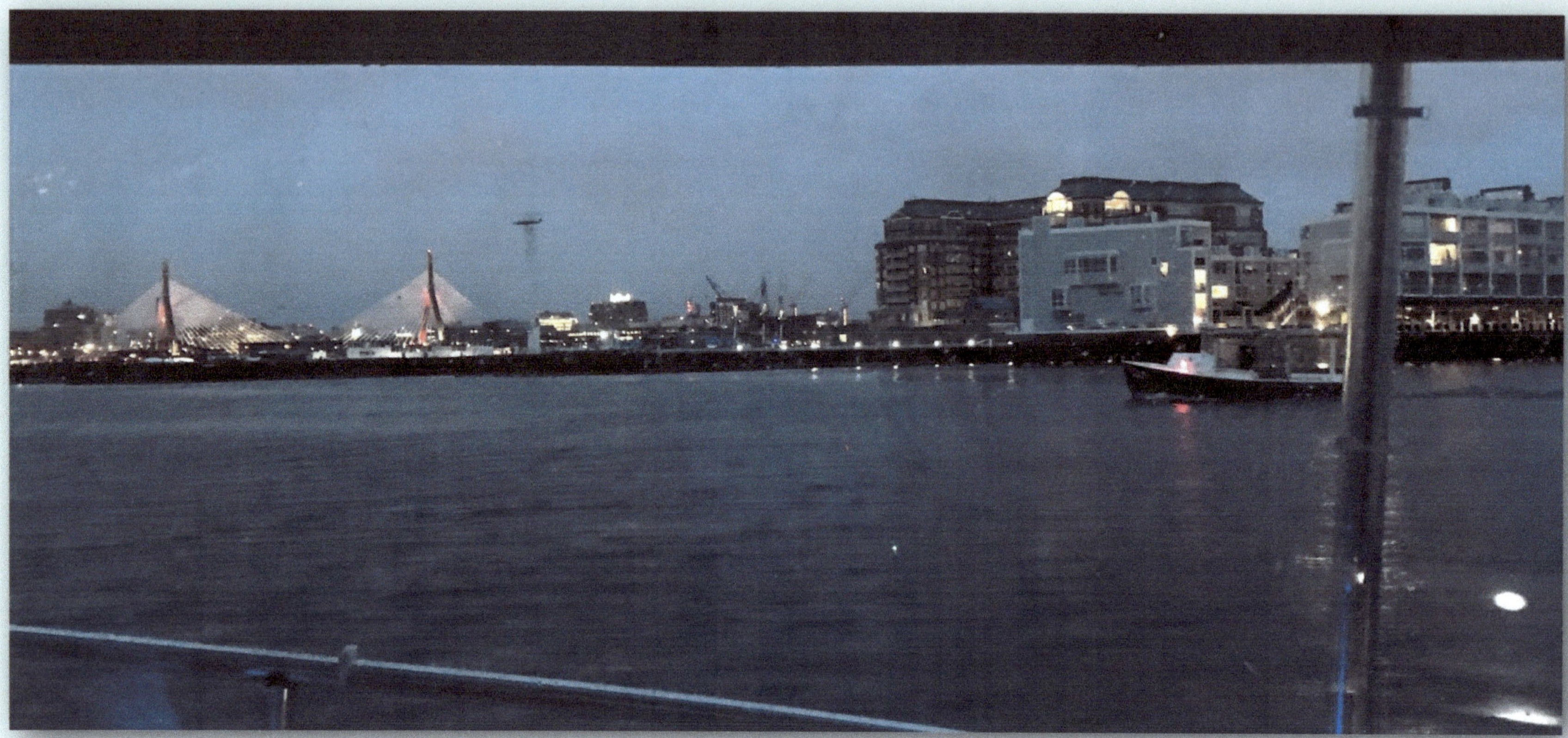

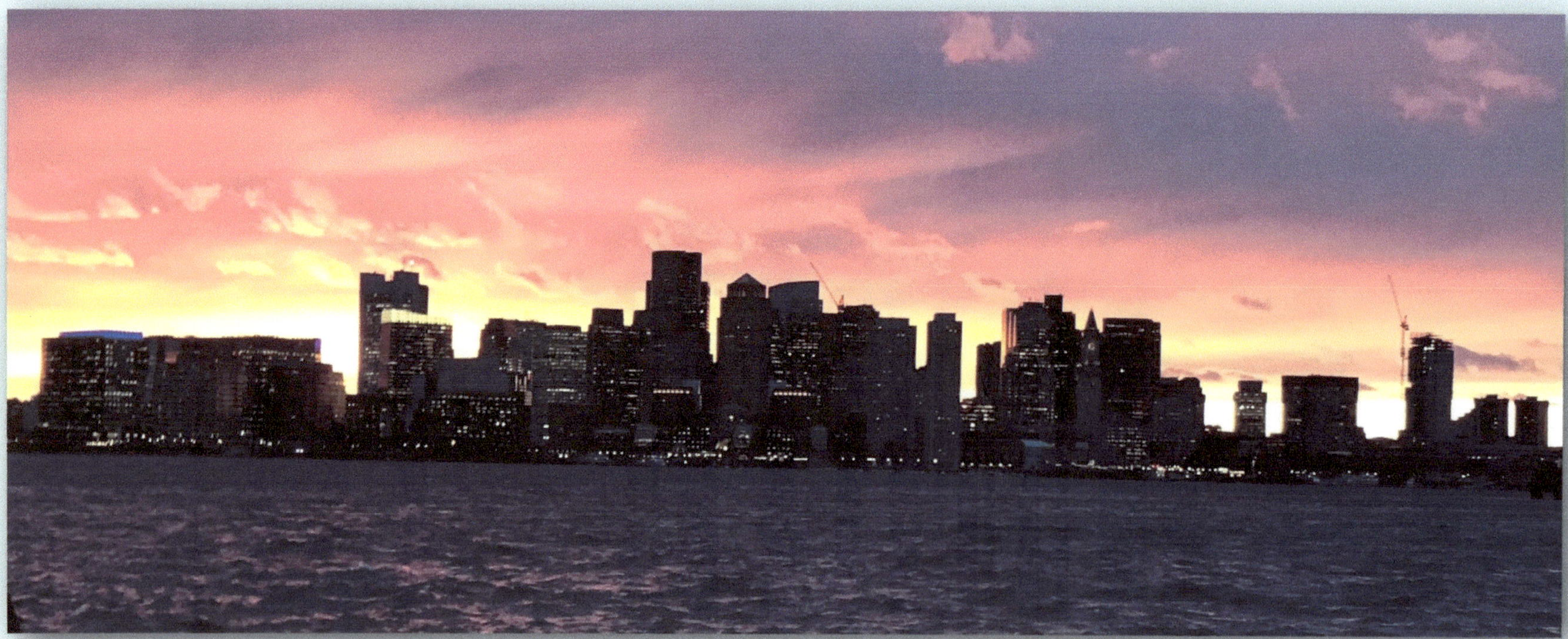

BIRDS, DUCKS & DUCKLINGS

At first this looked like a slalom water ski, with a cup on the back for the other foot. But turns out there are two bids snuggled on a large piece of driftwood. The large cranes of Conley Terminal used in *Star Wars* as walkers in background.

A pair of Canadian Geese, who mate for life. Around March and April they will have found a place to nest and lay and sit on the eggs until the goslings are ready to hatch.

LIFE ON THE HARBOR

109

ANDREA
BOSTON, MA
BONNIE
BOSTON

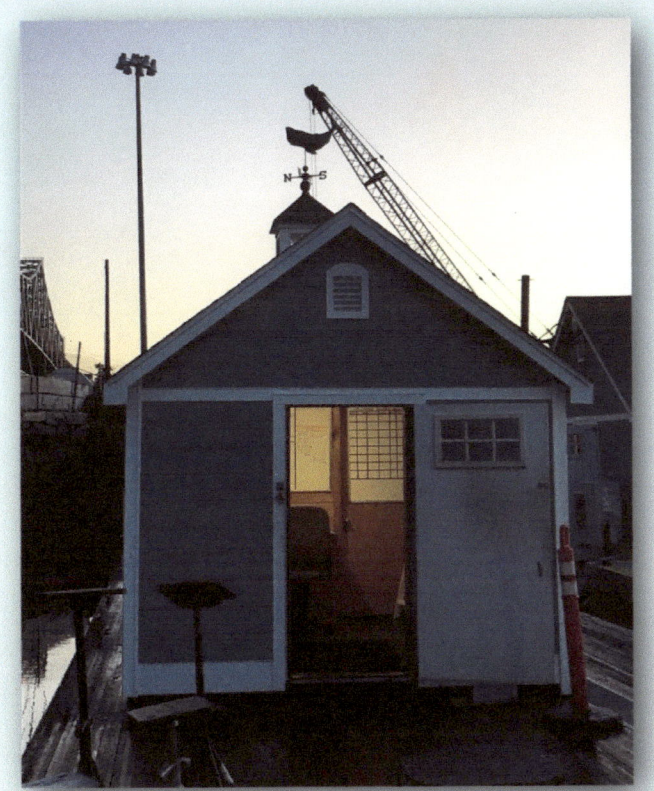

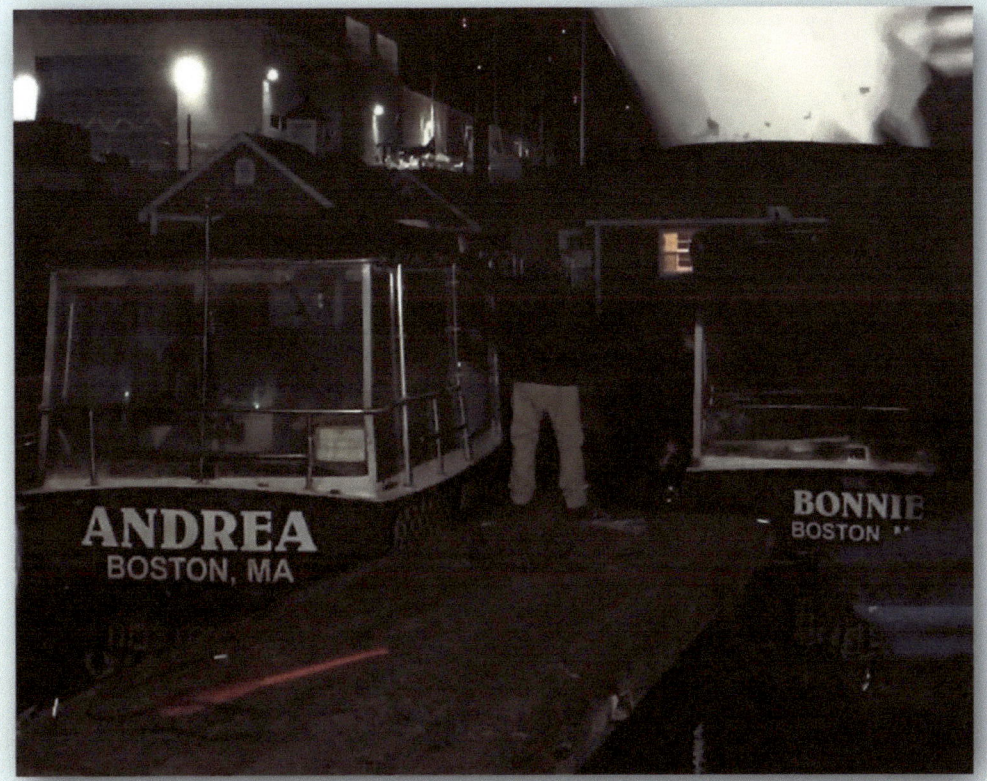

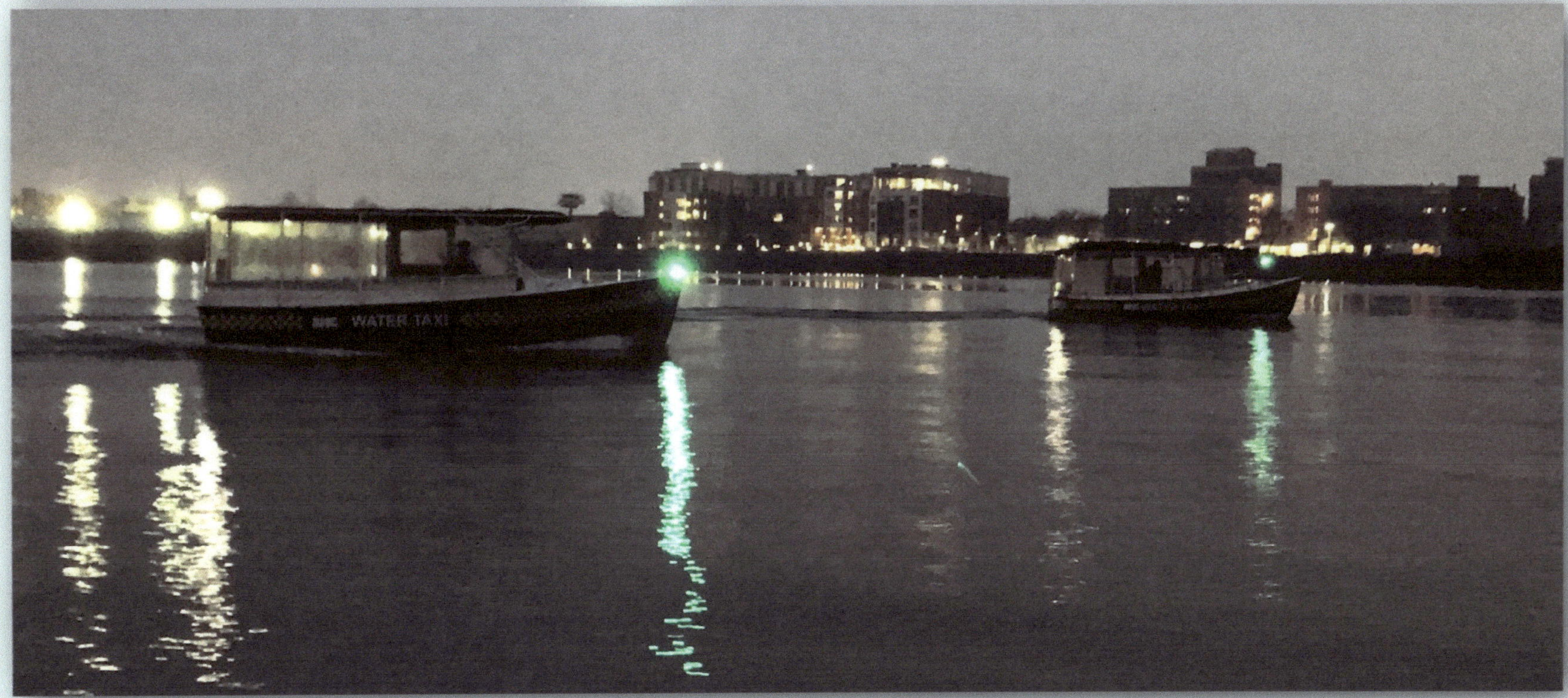
WATER TAXI

Two men seeming to walk on water swarmed Long Wharf one evening and asked the author to text them the footage he took of them.

Rearranging the salt pile in Chelsea Creek, on the Chelsea side of the McArdle Bridge.

Folks get around the harbor many ways.

Maintaining dozens of navigation lights on the old bridge trestle in Fort Point Channel; a cold, dirty job.

Spud and other barges bringing in heavy construction equipment to Seaport to improve the Harborwalk at the World Trade Center.

A passenger boat floating repair shed, a construction barge, and a clutch of lobster traps all share the same frame at Jeffries Point, Eastie, overlooking Southie and the Seaport.

Piers Park Sailing Center, where many of the boats are named after classic clippers designed and built in East Boston by Donald McKay.

USCG patrol craft having refueled.

The Boston Fuel Transportation pier in Eastie adjacent to The Eddy and ReelHouse restaurant.

After each watch, captains ensure there is no unreported damage, or attempt to repair same.

Not only do these men jackhammer away concrete and rebar sleeves, but they are also divers working underwater on the same pilons in winter.

Heading out for keelboat yacht racing from Constitution Marina, Charlestown, where many live-aboards spend the year afloat.

Captains confer

A summer gale reduced what had been a floating, moveable party palace into a shattered wreck in a few hours.

RANDOM SCENES ON BOSTON HARBOR

When work ceased on this construction barge in Fort Point Channel, all that was left was a port-a-potty and ropes around a tarp around some equipment.

Crew changes

Gangways on the floating jetty, Long Wharf North.

A butterfly nut on a sea strainer looking at a fan belt and a coolant fluid reservoir aboard a smaller vessel in the harbor.

The speedboat is a RIB (rigid inflatable boat) part of the small fleet belonging to the mega-yacht of an oligarch. The men in white shirts are officer and crew. The man in blue shirt is the owner or a guest who has just arrived at Logan and is about to be whisked across the harbor to Long Wharf, Boston Yacht Haven, the ICA waterfront, or Charlestown, where vessels with private security, several pools, numerous smaller boats and round-the-clock security tie up in the summer.

More floating debris; flotsam floats free from shore, jetsam is thrown into the sea from vessels. This would be flotsam and one piece can spend days or weeks in the harbor. No one group collects it year-round.

An Emirates A380 double-deck Airbus longhaul aircraft landing over Deer Island and Winthrop. The sailors anticipate their arrival to take advantage of drafts and the pilots say the planes are so large they create their own cushion effect when close to land.

This old navigation marker looks like it could have been a bomb of some sort as well.

A view with flotsam and jetsam from Eagle Hill, East Boston, looking at the auto terminal, Charlestown and the longest bridge in New England; the Tobin.

Logan International Airport takes up more land than East Boston and arguably than a large part of downtown Boston as well. Here planes take off over Jeffries Point and Winthrop.

Clockwise: Tunnel vents, USCG buoy tender, USCG helicopter, view from Eastie, and looking at the cargo cranes at the Conley Terminal which were said to have inspired George Lucas to create the enemy "walkers" in the Star Wars franchise.

East Boston at Border Street and Maverick Street.

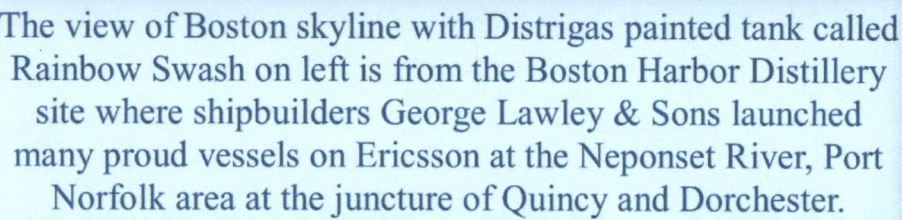

The view of Boston skyline with Distrigas painted tank called Rainbow Swash on left is from the Boston Harbor Distillery site where shipbuilders George Lawley & Sons launched many proud vessels on Ericsson at the Neponset River, Port Norfolk area at the juncture of Quincy and Dorchester.

Note the flamingo in the rigging!

New and old: ultra-modern sewage-treatment plant, and paper chart.

127

Navigational aids: Lights at Whidden Point, Eastie and across the way at Pier 4, Charlestown Navy Yard at the Courageous Sailing Center.

Water taxi captains must dock or undock countless times a day, alone, using their left hand to tie up and right hand to both steer and operate the throttle. Close attention and coordination is required so as not to lose digits.

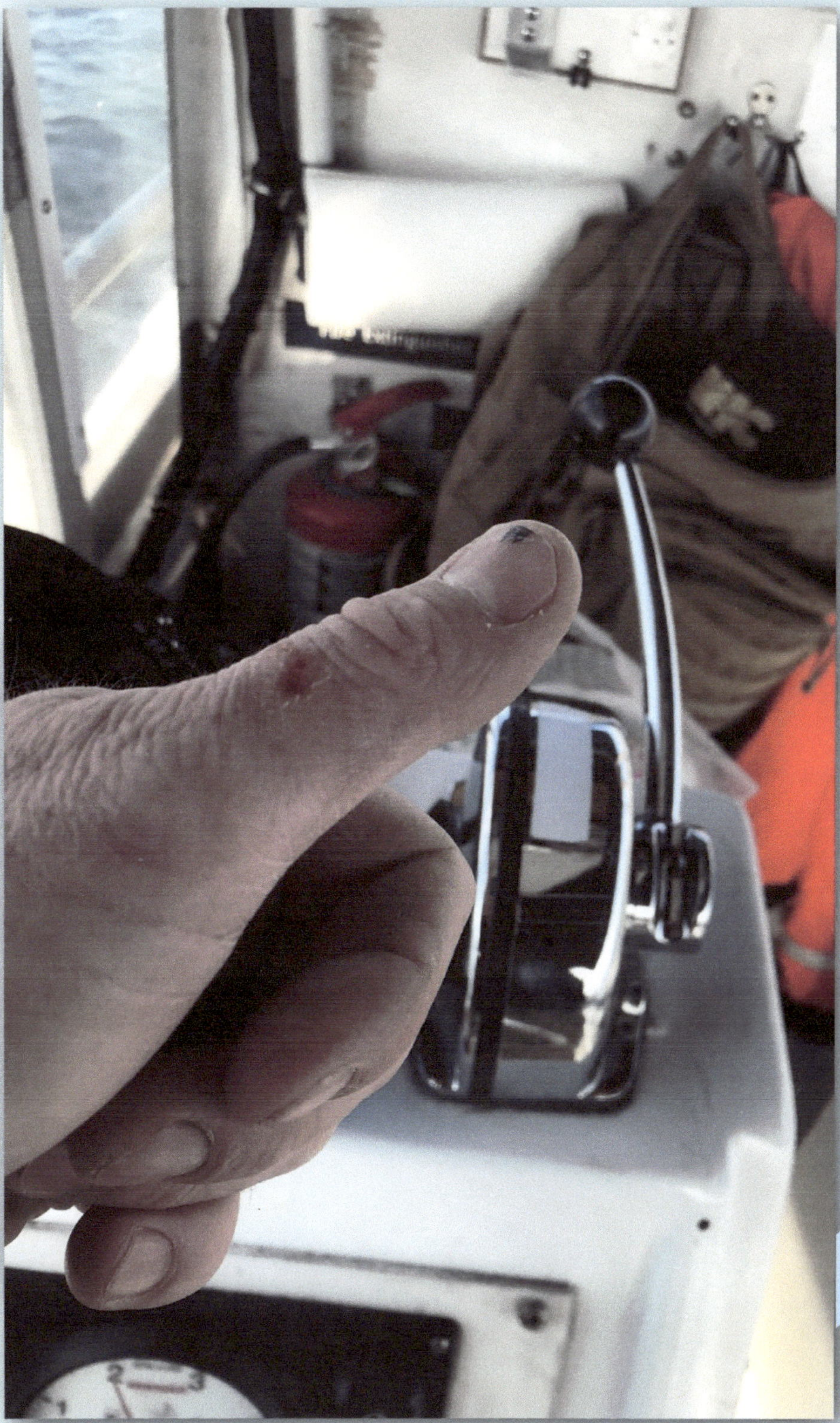

Courageous Sailing Office with Bunker Hill Monument, Charlestown.

What happens when roads and bollards don't get along.

Massport's VIP entertainment venue at the Fish Pier in the Seaport, which retains its grandeur.

Things that go "bump" in the night.

These pink buoys off the Boston Tea Party dock look official, however on closer inspection they are painted with children images and are bouncy balls for infants to sit on!

Union Wharf and nearby Sargents Wharf are some of the low-rise and parking-lot jetties that the public can enjoy like Pilot House Park without highrises looming over them.

131

Captains' quarters, Mystic.

Man overboard drill, required every month.

Feirce-looking bow of a passenger boat.

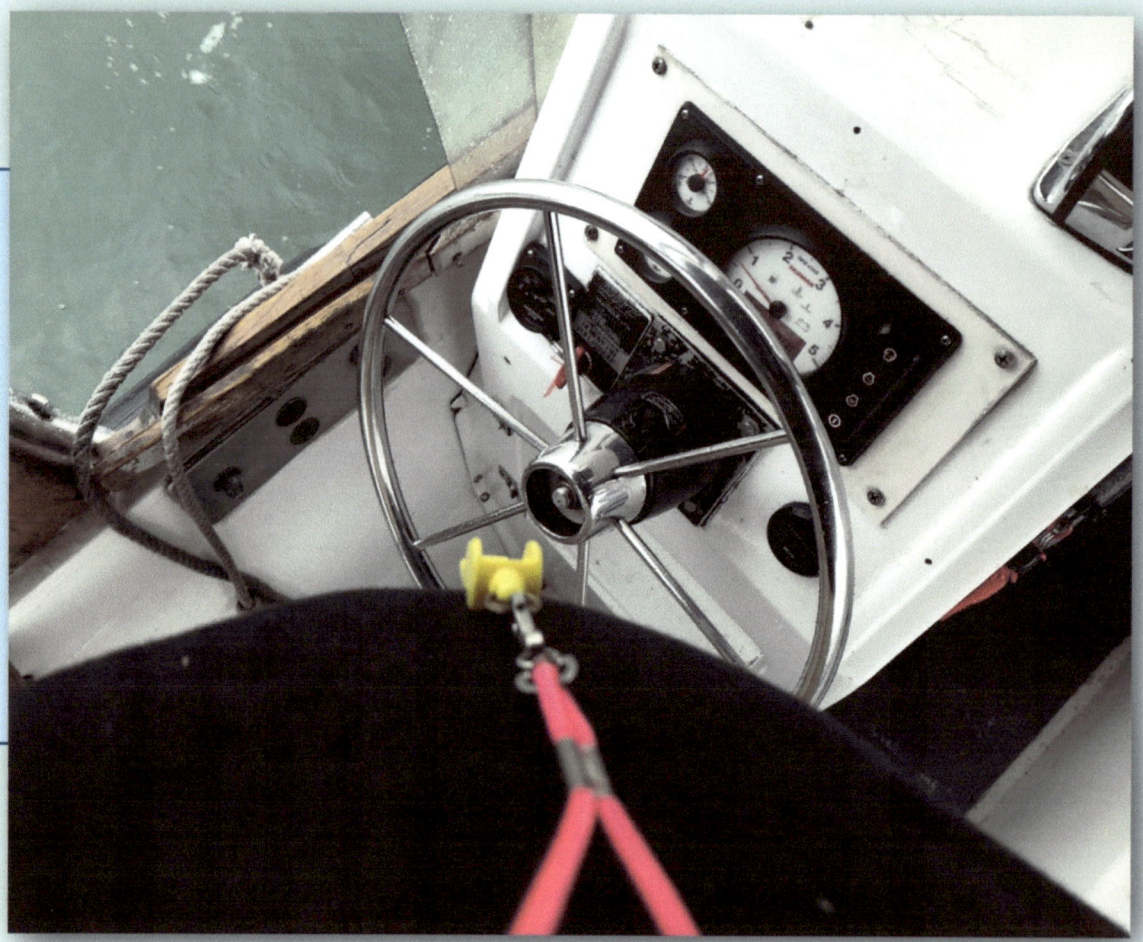

Steering console with window enabling the captain to tie the boat up. Whistle is in the event of another Man Overboard (MOB) incident, as author was once lost oveboard in a snowstorm for 16 minutes off Block Island.

How to make a salt pile cheerful! The Chelsea Creek salt pile adorned with illuminated Santa and reindeer in December.

The author's mother's name is Jane, so this flotsam seems fortuitous! Stormy conditions, and kids do sometime leave their hallmark, as with this pirate ship sticker left aboard a boat.

Not to be outshone by the Institute of Contemporary Art and determined to be accessible to everyone, commercial and recreational divers in East Boston have created a unique "Boston SCUBA [self contained underwater breathing apparatus] Museum and Gift Shop." It consists of hundreds or more priceless or useless bits of ephemera dug off the seabed of Boston Harbor and placed generously on display on a dock, free of charge, open around the clock! This trust system seems to work.

This is a plate from "The Cunard Steamship Company, Ltd."! Winch handles, chamber pots, and odds and ends. Sir Samuel Cunard, of Halifax, is said to have asked King George V of England to name a ship after "England's greatest queen," meaning Victoria. The king replied that "it is lovely of you to name your ship after my wife, Mary!"

These industrial-strength cast-iron bollards on a deteriorated railway peir at Jeffries Point have come unhinged and appear to be dancing with each other.

This is a Carley Float, famously used in mass quantities in World War II, which saved countless lives as it did not have to be launched, but mostly just popped free from sinking ships. One disadvantage was the need for legs or much of the body to be immersed. This one is in disuse but you can still find them on some US-flagged ships, which due to a century-old cabotage rule named the Jones Act, are very expensive to replace.

WINTER ON BOSTON HARBOR

In the snow, exchanging equipment and having a gam

The *Thompson Island* Outward Bound vessel passing an outbound ATB.

Where is the captain? He or she just assumed command and is performing quick safety checks.

Docks need to be kept snow-free. Water taxis arrive at 5.45 am, so often their captains jump in whether they "have" to or not.

An offshore wind vessel from the US Gulf in Mystic Channel, under the Tobin Bridge in Charlestown.

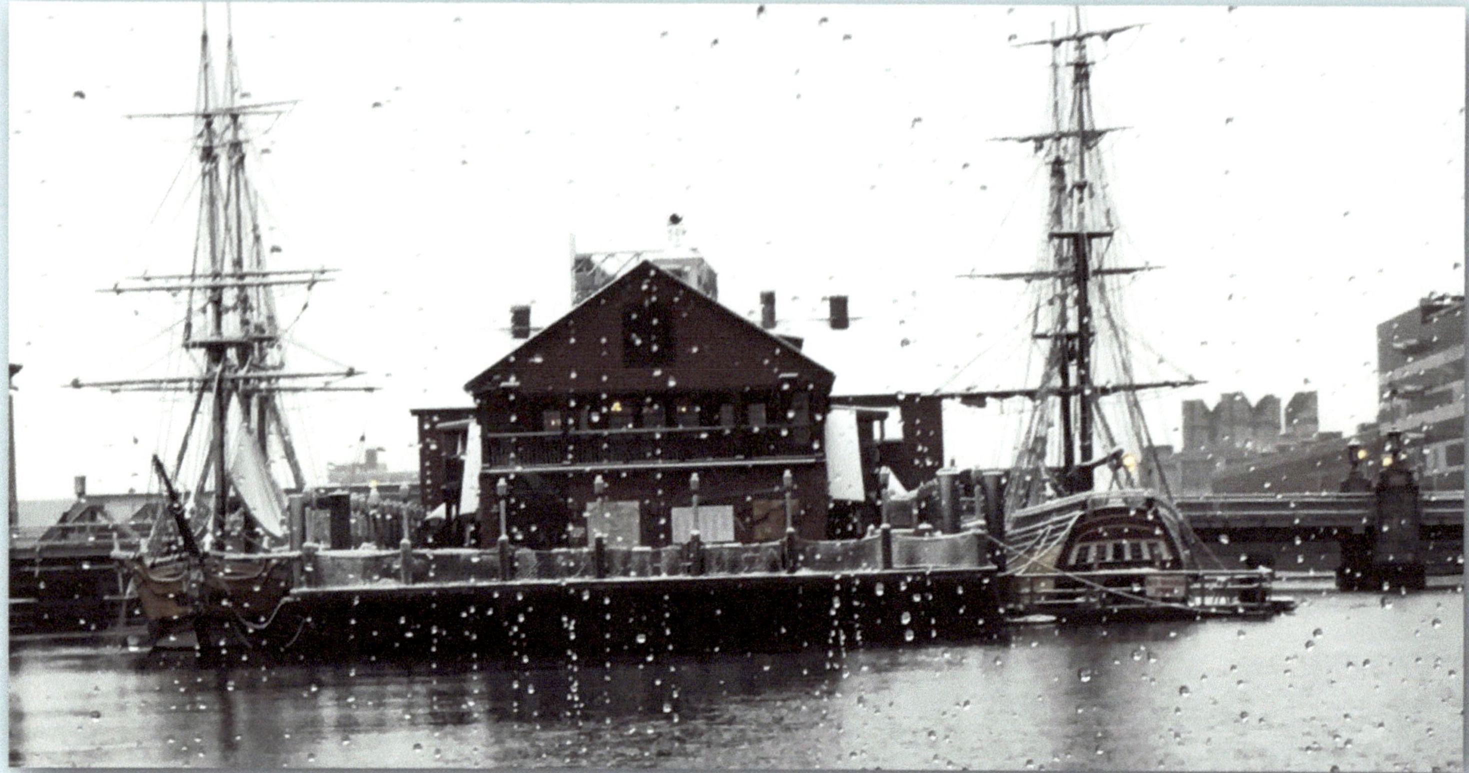

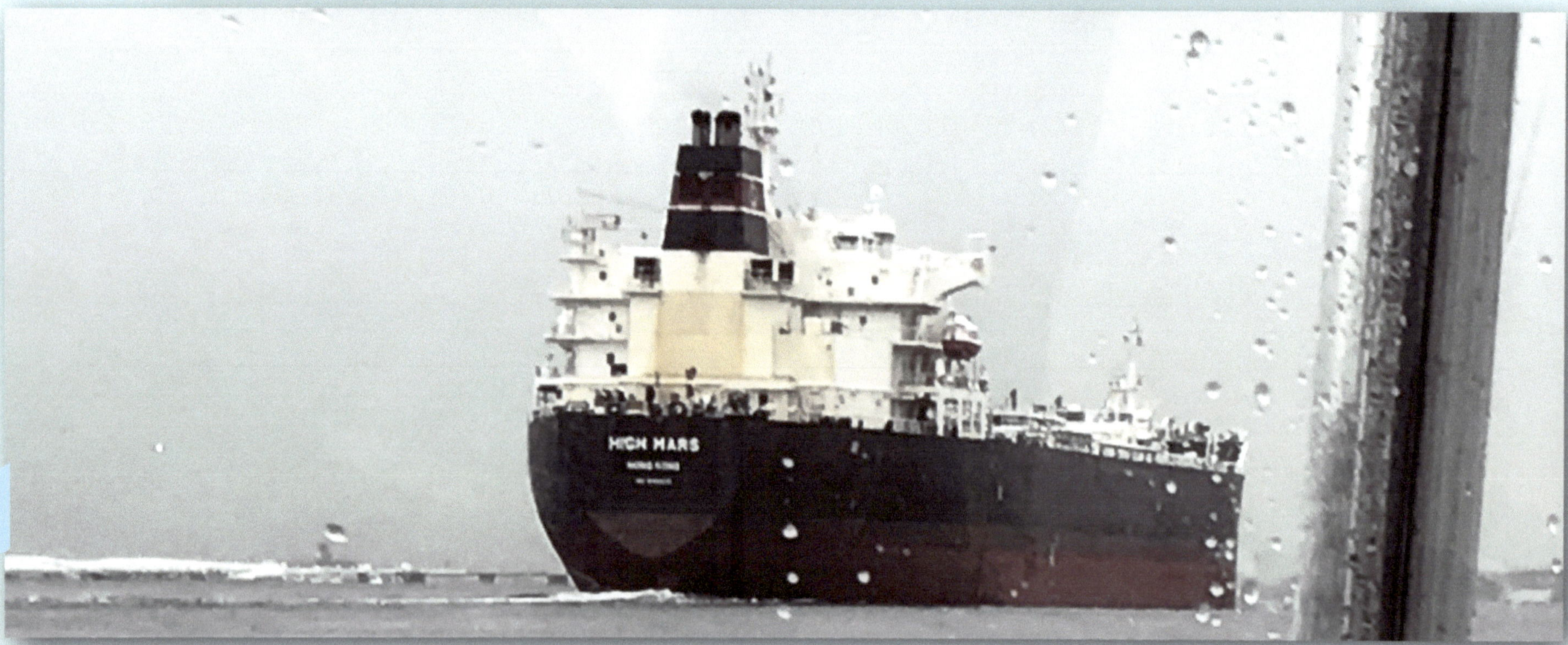
HIGH MARS

At the Moakley US Courthouse, viewing the redundant, now historic original bridge, now replaced by the Seaport Boulevard.

A gas tanker arriving left, a large tanker named *High Mars* on the right. Flagged to Hong Kong and built in 2009, the oil and chemical tanker can carry 51,500 tons of cargo.

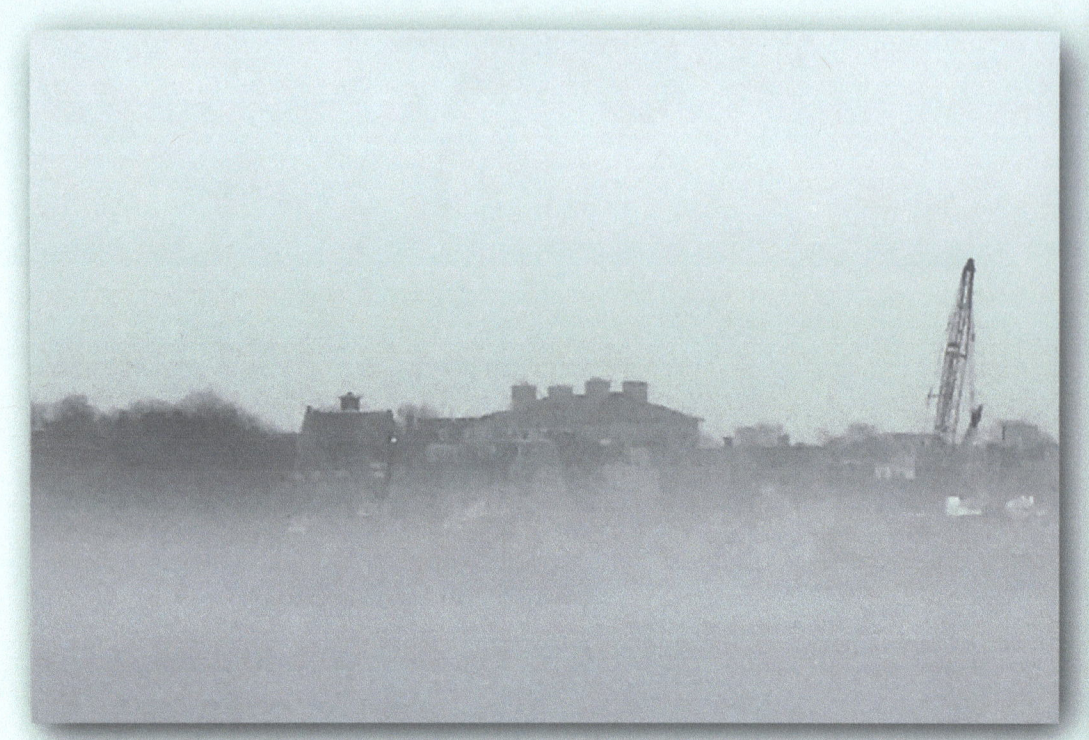

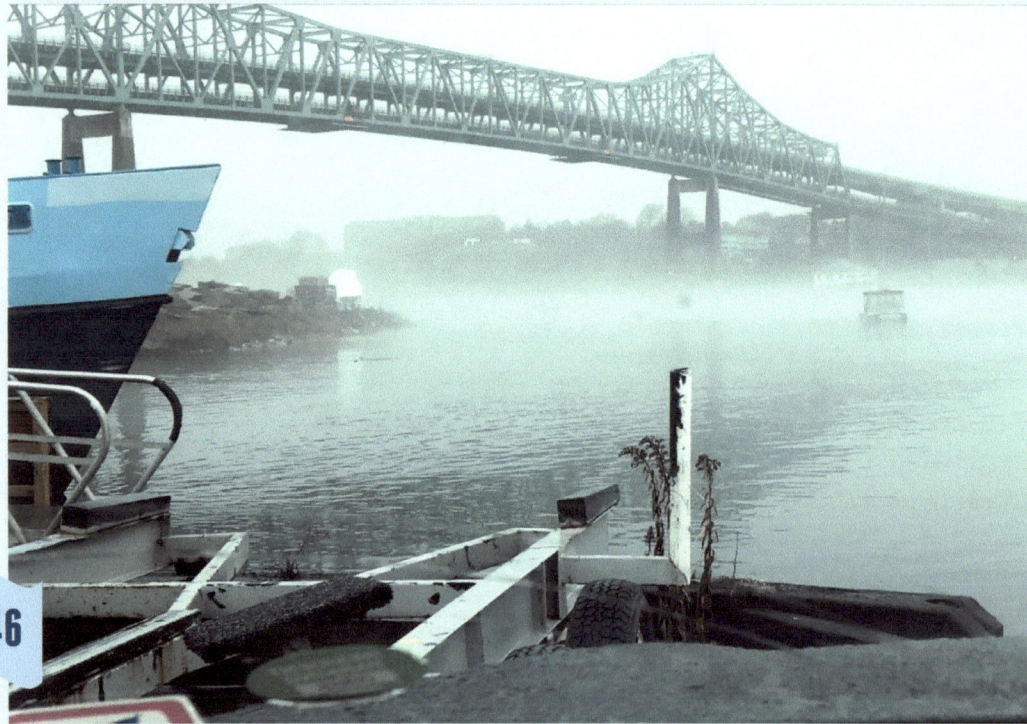

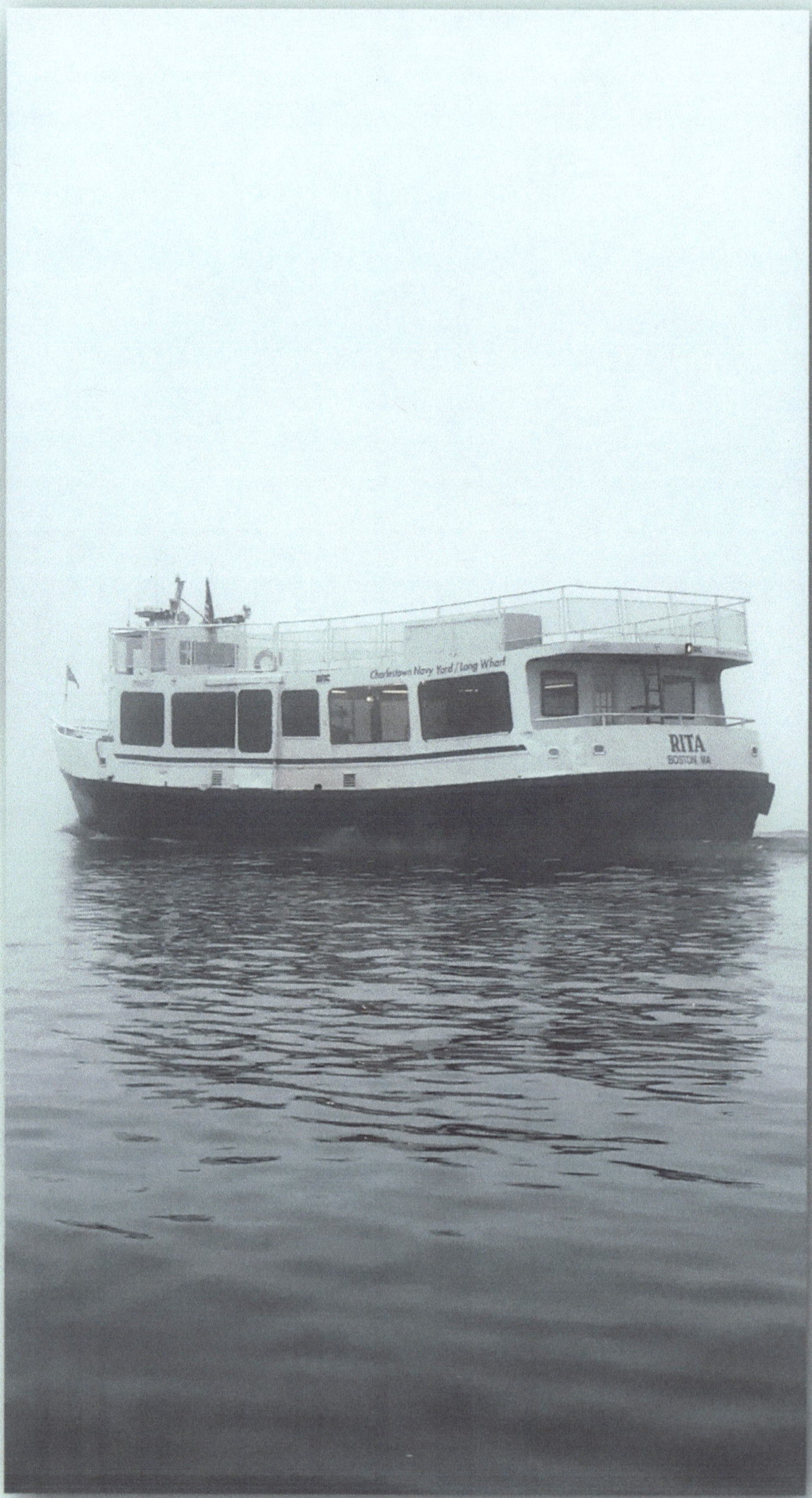
Charlestown Navy Yard / Long Wharf
RITA
BOSTON, MA

Winnisimmet Street, Chelsea, looking across the harbor to downtown Boston, and North End.

151

EAST BOSTON

Boston Towing & Transportation (Reinauer) wharves, White Street and Border Street, where Donald McKay built dozens of world class clipper ships et. al. over 25 years.

Eastie to the left, Boston skyline left center, Charlestown and Tobin right center, Chelsea right and housing towers of Shore Plaza East at far right.

West side of the Bang Corporation property, bordering the Mobil station.

Yacht on props at Bang Corporation

Main office shack and entrance to Bang Corporation, home of 100 or so vessels in various states of repair.

In the cleft formed by the southwest terminus of the McArdle Bridge and the Bang Corporation property in Eastie.

These three power boats with fine lines and bows bring a certain poise and elegance to an otherwise chaotic-looking scene.

In the distance, from left is the Chelsea Yacht Club, Global Petroleum where sizeable tankers as well as barges discharge and bunker barges load, on Broadway in Chelsea, Admirals Hill former US Navy installation, now residential units, in background. To right the vessels in slipways and tied up, like the historic tug *Luna*, are in the Fitzgerald Shipyard on Ferry Street.

In foreground to left a USCG Surfboat rescue craft. In middle ground a Sea Tow commercial rescue vessel towing a smallish houseboat probably to its summer home in a marina closer to Boston, probably to Charlestown Marina or Constitution Marina. In the background, from right to left is: East Somerville and a MBTA assembly and garage facility (out of sight) on Gardner Street, on the Mystic River, the Schrafft's candy firm, several industrial piers in Charlestown with a lot of aggregate barge activity, the Wind Technology Testing Center for that burgeoning industry, dock aprons for huge wind turbine blades, and for many thousands of imported cars to be parked and staged, the Boston Harbor Cruises Autoport dispatch center and offices, Portside Truck and Auto Repair, Boston Boatworks, and the large concrete silos underneath the Tobin Bridge which are for receiving gypsum rock for the construction (dry-wall) industries, and owned by the United States Gypsum Company. Ships that berth right there must be geared, or self-unloading type. Directly above the white houseboat in this image one can see the contraptions set up to receive the cargo, and there are systems in place to mitigate dust and prevent moisture from reaching the cargo. The large tan building to left is for automobile processing from ship to trucking rig, etc. and includes dormitories and many automotive bays.

Tug *Luna* is historic, having been built of wood in 1930 and with her sister tug *Venus* was one of the most powerful in the US. A veteran of service for the US Navy in World War II, shuttling ships via the Cape Cod Canal, (which suffered a ship aground and stuck, that had to be blown up as other ships were sunk by U-boats rounding the cape), she was abandoned on the Charles River until restored faithfully 2007 to 2010. Her saviors are the Tug *Luna* Preservation Society.

The salt pile at Eastern Minerals in Chelsea, bounded by Chelsea Creek, Marginal Street and the McArdle Bridge. No salt pile received as many bulk shipments from so many ships: Greek, Japanese, Chinese, Italian, Canadian and so on, yet because 2019-2020 was a mild, warm winter overall the pile of product from either Bahamas, Chile, Egypt or all three remained tall as you can see.

McArdle Bridge looking south, is named for a community leader. Boat, tug, ship captains and pilots hear the bridge operator at all hours day and night. I believe I've seen a fishing pole hanging from a window, but may have been mistaken!

A creek in Chelsea bordered by Wharf Street, Winnisimmet Street, Marginal Street, and Pearl Street as it becomes Andrew McArdle Bridge. It's always lovely finding beaches in urban areas, and there were a number of them in this area.

Eastern Minerals salt piles being re-arranged.

PORT Park, another aggregate or mineral bulk facility.

The men in this workboat are waiting for the two tugs to be broken down and to support and assist the pushboat, the barges, the cranes or all three. The goose is just gliding by.

The 1940-built tug *Gaspee*, it's starboard bow already badly damaged and partially flooded from being just dumped at the waterfront months before, is laying partially on its side as nearby another condemned tug is cut to bits by a crane. Named for a major revolutionary event in which John Brown and Abraham Whipple of Profidence led the attack on and torching of a grounded British customs schooner named *HMS Gaspee* on June 9, 1772. This tug was sold to Acushnet Marine Inc. and within a few hours of this photo being taken was probably cut up, placed on a barge, shifted to the scrap metal yard in Everett or elsewhere, and may well end up being repurposed for a startup venture in a developing economy. Steel considered "pre nuclear" has a better resale market to some buyers.

Gaspee to the left as its colleague is broken up with Eagle Hill, East Boston to the right.

Here the bollards, or bits used to tie lines and wires, are clearly visible on the deck of the tug being destroyed. In the background is the modern Chelsea Creek Bridge in the raised position, which can be seen from Saugus, Revere, Melrose and other suburbs to the north as well as Winthrop to the east.

Men walking past the carcass of a tug, with the taffrail or stern elliptical and grey visible on the earth the left. Ahead is the international salt pile, with hints of pink, suggesting the salt is solar from the salt pans of the Morton Salt facility at Mathew Town, Great Inagua, southern Bahamas (the author once rode a ship, the CSL *Atlantic Erie*, which loaded 40,000 tons of salt from Inagua to Norfolk and New York). The pink color comes from the same natural dye canthaxanthin which turns flamingos from being grey at birth to pink from their diet of blue-green algae and brine shrimp.

Houseboats; some of many liveaboard vessels at Boston Bay Marina off Condor Street in East Boston between Eagle Hill and on Chelsea Creek.

The Boston Towing tug *Freedom* guiding a chemical or petroleum barge being pushed by the Kirby Marine tug *Denali* from Chelsea Creek through the McArdle Bridge past the PORT Park in Chelsea. If it looks this narrow, we must recall that large tankers and bulkers of up to 50,000 cargo tons through the same bridges and channels.

Left to right: Power cruiser at Bang Corporation on Nay, Condor, and Meridian streets, another power boat, this one wrapped in plastic for winterization, at Boston Bay Marina, Condor Street, then a yellow pushboat with elevated bridge supporting demolition of a tug on Nay Street. Above that is the elevated bridge of the Kirby Corporation tug *Denali*, beneath which (no relation) is the battered small tug named *Success* at Bang. Between all of this is the McArdle Bridge, with Tobin Bridge in background, and Global Petroleum in Chelsea backed by Distrigas and other energy facilities in Everett in the distance. So 5 boats, 2 bridges, 2 marinas, 2 energy plants and a wind turbine and three towns in one photo.

Two bridges, two tugs, one barge and many patient cars whose drivers wait to transit to and from Eastie and Chelsea.

BOSTON HARBOR ON THE EVE OF THE CORONAVIRUS LOCKDOWN

Distributing supplies to ward off or minimalize the spread of contagion.

"Where the Harbor Comes to Life" reads the huge white banner in the arch to left for the Boston Marriott Long Wharf. Sadly the entire frontage is boarded up by yellow barricades. Columbus Park is completely void of people in the middle of a usually busy workday with clear and mild mid-March weather as the city entered lockdown. The following day radios were retrieved and all passenger vessel activities were halted. Soon only USCG, state, town, city police and fire departments and Massport and environmental police would be patrolling the waters. Harbor dolphins, myriad species of birds, whales, seals, sharks will likely move closer into the harbor in the absence of hundreds of vessels.

Rowes Wharf and the Financial District as seen from Fan Pier and the John Joseph Moakley US Courthouse. The following day the purr and roar of vessel engines in Boston Harbor largely fell silent. Good night, Boston.

ABOUT THE AUTHOR

Eric Wiberg has lived in New England for thirty years. In 1983, he moved to Massachusetts from the Bahamas for boarding school, then to Newport, which was his home-port for fifteen years. He became a yacht captain (US Merchant Marine license, 1995), obtained a maritime law degree (2004), and a masters in marine affairs (2005), the same year he was admitted to the bar in the Commonwealth of Massachusetts. The founder of Echo Yacht Delivery (1999), Wiberg has sailed over 125 vessels from Maine to Long Island and globally in over 60 countries. A Boston College graduate, he has lived or worked in Camden, Norwalk, Westport, and Charlestown. He studied geography in Oxford, law in Lisbon, and film in New York. The author of over 20 books, his focus is on maritime casualties. Having commercially operated a tanker fleet from Singapore, he worked in maritime recruiting and media sales in Stamford, Connecticut, and the ship-docking industry in New York City, where he was born. In the spring of 2019 he moved to East Boston to be closer to son and co-author, Felix, assuming a full-time, year-round role on Boston Harbor in August.

www.ingramcontent.com/pod-product-compliance
Lightning Source LLC
Chambersburg PA
CBHW050855010526
44118CB00005BA/176